HER STORY, HER STRENGTH

50 GOD-EMPOWERED WOMEN OF THE BIBLE

SARAH PARKER RUBIO

To Daddy, who first introduced me to these women, and
to the One who created, loved, and empowered them.

And to Aurora Sofía, my beautiful gift—may
you always know how much you are loved.

—SPR

ZONDERKIDZ

Her Story, Her Strength
Copyright © 2023 by Sarah E. Rubio
Illustrations © 2023 by Zondervan

Requests for information should be addressed to:
Zonderkidz, *3900 Sparks Dr. SE, Grand Rapids, Michigan 49546*

ISBN 978-0-310-14431-1 (hardcover)
ISBN 978-0-310-14435-9 (audio download)
ISBN 978-0-310-14436-6 (ebook)

Library of Congress Cataloging-in-Publication Data

Names: Rubio, Sarah Parker, author. | Williams, Anastasia Magloire, illustrator.
Title: Her story, her strength : 50 God-empowered women of the Bible / Sarah Parker Rubio, Anastasia Magloire Williams.
Description: Grand Rapids : Zonderkidz, 2023. | Audience: Ages 8-12 | Summary: "Girls are beautifully and wonderfully made in God's image. This comprehensive collection of stories focused on 50 women of the Bible shows how God worked in their lives and continues to have a plan and a purpose for his beloved daughters today. In a world that too often tells girls that they are not enough, Her Story, Her Strength uses biblical retellings and reflections that include the historical context behind each story to remind young women that they have a God who loves them deeply and empowers them to live and love like he does. For any girl ages 8 and up who is asking questions about her worth, identity, and place in the world and church, this colorful and engaging book provides a positive, loving, and scriptural lens that helps them interpret the messages they receive from their peers, media, and society"— Provided by publisher.
Identifiers: LCCN 2022029974 (print) | LCCN 2022029975 (ebook) | ISBN 9780310144311 (hardcover) | ISBN 9780310144366 (ebook)
Subjects: LCSH: Women in the Bible—Juvenile literature. | BISAC: JUVENILE NONFICTION / Religion / Biblical Biography
Classification: LCC BS575 .R75 2023 (print) | LCC BS575 (ebook) | DDC 220.9/2082—dc23/eng/20220808
LC record available at https://lccn.loc.gov/2022029974
LC ebook record available at https://lccn.loc.gov/2022029975

Published in association with the literary agency of Credo Communications LLC., Grand Rapids, Michigan; www.credocommunications.net.

Zonderkidz is a trademark of Zondervan.

Zondervan titles may be purchased in bulk for educational, business, fundraising, or sales promotional use. For information, please email SpecialMarkets@Zondervan.com.

Art direction: Cindy Davis
Cover and interior illustrations: Anastasia Magloire Williams
Interior Design: Denise Froehlich

Printed in Malaysia

23 24 25 26 27   IMG   10 9 8 7 6 5 4 3 2 1

CONTENTS

AUTHOR'S NOTE

In this book, you will read fifty stories about women from the Bible. Some of their names may be familiar to you, while you may learn about others for the first time (and a few of the women aren't even named in Scripture!). Some of their stories take up multiple chapters in the Bible while others are mentioned in only one or two verses. But all of these women were important to God, and all of them can teach us something about who he is and how he works.

Each woman's story is divided into three sections. "Her Story" is a retelling of all or part of the biblical narrative in which she appears, imagining what it was like to experience the world through her eyes. I did my best to be faithful and accurate to the details that are given about each woman in the Bible while expanding the story to help you picture what she might have been like. I also let you know what facts are not given in Scripture. That's where "Her World" comes in. This section contains interesting historical facts and ideas from Bible scholars about the woman, her land and culture, and the meaning of her biblical story. (I would not have been able to write this section without the excellent work of many smart people who have spent years studying the Bible and its history. Big thanks to all of them!) Most importantly, "Her God" talks about what we can learn about God from each woman's story.

As I wrote this book, I found myself thinking over and over, *God really loves women and girls!* I hope you feel the same as you read.

EVE

STRONG IN HIS IMAGE

God created human beings in his own image. In the image
of God he created them; male and female he created them.

GENESIS 1:27, NLT

⟶⟫⟫⟫| HER STORY |⟪⟪⟪⟵

The woman opened her eyes and stared into the vast, beautiful space she would soon learn to call the sky. Bright colors and wondrous sights she didn't yet have names for swirled all around her—green leaves, blue streams, warm golden sunlight, juicy red fruit. She breathed in, enjoying the feeling of her chest expanding and the delicious smells that tickled her nose. She found she could wiggle her fingers and her toes, and sit up, then stand. She stretched her hands high above her head. It felt good to move! The woman caught movement out of the corner of her eye and realized she wasn't alone. Brightly feathered creatures perched in the trees, and lithe, velvety shapes crept through the tall grass. After watching them for a while, the woman realized they were alive and awake, like her. They were beautiful and wonderful, but they were not of her kind. *Is there anyone else like me?* she wondered.

But the woman didn't feel lonely or worried or afraid. Everything in her new home was wonderful and perfect and full of joy. Best of all, God was right there beside her. The woman knew that God had made her. He was her Father. He loved her and said she was one of the best things he had ever created—made in his image. And she wasn't the only one!

God led her to the man—later, he would be called Adam. He was lying down, sleeping. He opened his eyes and saw the woman—later, she would be called Eve—for the very first time. Adam smiled. "At last!" he said. "You are like me—flesh of my flesh and bone of my bone." Adam told Eve that God had said it wasn't good for Adam to be alone. God had brought every kind of animal to Adam, and the man had named each one. While Adam loved all the animals, none of them was the right partner for him. He needed someone like himself—someone made in God's very own image. "This is very good," God said. "Together, you will take care of the beautiful world I have made."

➤➤➤| HER WORLD |⟵⟵⟵

The Bible doesn't tell us exactly what it was like for Eve right after she was created, so we can't know for sure what Eve's world was like, but the Bible does tell us a few interesting things. We know she lived in a world that was fresh and new and perfect. Nothing had yet been broken by sin or damaged by people's bad decisions. The Bible also talks about a river that flowed out of Eden and the various lands the branches of that river flowed through. People have different ideas about where those might appear on a modern map—suggestions include Egypt, Armenia, or somewhere in the Middle East.

The Bible also tells us that God planted a garden in Eden for Adam and Eve to live in. He lovingly made a beautiful home for them and taught them how to care for it. We know God planted many delicious fruit trees to produce food for his beloved children. And God himself walked with them in the garden every evening.

Eve lived in God's garden with Adam and the animals in perfect peace, joy, and harmony. Many people believe there were no such things as wild animals—all of God's creatures trusted and loved Adam and Eve like our pets trust and love us today. Some people even believe that animals could talk, since Eve didn't seem surprised when the serpent spoke to her. Of course, we can't know that for sure, but it's an interesting idea!

⟶≫| HER GOD |≪⟵

Because our Bibles use the pronouns "he" or "him" for God, people often think of God as a man. But God is not male or female the way humans are. The Bible says he made *all* human beings—boys and girls, men and women—in his image. This doesn't mean our bodies look like God's—he is Spirit and doesn't have a physical body like we do. Genesis 1 uses two Hebrew words to describe how humans are made in God's image. One of the words, *tselem*, is often used with statues or models. God intended us to be replicas of himself. He gave us many of his own characteristics—like the ability to love and to create—though we are limited in ways that God isn't. The second Hebrew word, *demut*, means "to be like or to resemble." One of the ways God made us to be like him is in the job he gave us of ruling creation as his representatives.

Sadly, Eve is famous not only for being the first woman who ever lived, but also for being the first person who ever disobeyed God. When Adam and Eve sinned—chose their own way over God's—the image of God in them, and in all the humans who came after them, was broken. But it would be a mistake to give Eve's story a sad ending. Right after God told Adam and Eve about the consequences of their sin, he told them how he would save them from sin and its consequences—by sending his Son, Jesus. The Bible calls Jesus the second Adam. He accomplished what the first Adam couldn't—perfect obedience to God—and gave us a chance to have a new life and to act like the image bearers we were meant to be. Being made in God's image means that he works through us to accomplish what he wants to do in the world. Even if, like Eve, we make terrible choices, God doesn't want our story to end there. He wants to save us from the brokenness of the world, and the brokenness inside us. Through his power, and through bearing his image, you can be strong!

> READ ABOUT EVE IN GENESIS 1:26–4:26.

HAGAR

STRONG AND SEEN

Hagar used another name to refer to the Lord, who had spoken to her. She said, "You are the God who sees me."

GENESIS 16:13, NLT

→»»| HER STORY |«««-

Hagar sank to her knees beside the spring. Her tears had long since dried on her face, but her hands still shook so much as she scooped water into them that she spilled as much as she drank. It was a long time before she was able to drink enough to stop her thirst.

Hagar huddled in the shade of a windblown tree and wrapped her arms around her belly. The baby inside her kicked hard enough to make her gasp. She wondered if he could tell they were in a strange place, far from the familiar sounds of her master Abram's camp and the movements of Hagar's daily routine. Could the baby hear her groans and feel her chest heaving with sobs? Was he frightened too? Hagar rubbed the spot where her baby was kicking and tried to calm her breathing.

Hagar regretted allowing herself to believe that Abram would favor her over his wife of so many years simply because Hagar was carrying his only child—the son he believed was part of a promise from his God. She regretted even more giving in to the temptation to treat her mistress, Sarai, like a secondary wife. Sarai's revenge had been quick and harsh. Hagar's body ached with bruises, and Sarai's angry words felt like they had been burned across her heart and mind. Sarai had made Hagar's life so miserable that she'd felt she had no choice but to run away. Now she was alone in the desert, pregnant, and on the run. She would be an easy target for anyone who came along—if she didn't die from hunger or thirst or fall prey to a wild animal first.

"Hagar." She looked around wildly. Had someone from Abram's camp noticed her escape and followed her? But she didn't recognize the person who had spoken. His voice was gentle—it had been so long since anyone had said her name with kindness—but he seemed to carry a power and authority that made it hard to look at him.

"Servant of Sarai, where have you come from, and where are you going?"

Hagar gulped. If he knew she was Sarai's servant, there was no point in lying. She was too tired and frightened to make up a convincing story anyway. She took a deep breath. "I am running away from Sarai." She wanted to explain, to tell him about the beatings and insults, the bruises and tears. But she knew he wouldn't care. No one cared about a servant's feelings. Sarai ruled over Hagar's life as absolutely as the pharaoh reigned over Egypt, her home country. When Sarai had ordered Hagar to become Abram's servant wife and have a child with him, Hagar had no choice. When her baby was born, Hagar was supposed to simply hand him over, and Sarai would raise him as her own. And when Sarai wanted to treat Hagar harshly, Hagar was supposed to endure it without a single complaint. This stranger would think she was a criminal for running away.

The stranger was quiet for a long time, so long that Hagar couldn't stand it anymore. She risked peeking at his face. He was looking at her, but not with judgment or harshness. His gaze was soft and kind, like he knew what she'd been through, all her sadness and anger, all the wrong and unfair things that had been done to her.

"Go back to Sarai and be a faithful servant to her," the stranger said. Hagar's heart sank. She must have only imagined the kindness in his eyes. But then the stranger said, "I will give you more descendants than you can count."

What? How many times had she overheard Abram talking about that same kind of promise from his God? Who was this person?

"Soon you will have a son," the stranger said. "You should name him Ishmael, because God has heard your cries of sadness."

Ishmael—"God hears." Could it be true? Had God heard her? Hagar thought about all the times she'd hid her tears from Sarai and Abram and the other servants, all the times she'd cried as silently as she could while everyone slept. She had run away because no one was on her side or cared what happened to her. But God had sent a messenger just to tell her he'd heard her and to promise that her son would be a great man—and that she would be the mother of a nation.

Hagar sat for a long time after God's messenger disappeared, lost in wonder. Finally, she bowed her head. "You are the God who sees me," she prayed. Then she got up and turned toward Abram's camp. She didn't know what kind of welcome would be waiting for her there, but she knew that whatever happened, she would be heard and cared for and known by the God who saw her.

→»»| HER WORLD |«««‑

As a servant in Bible times, Hagar's status was very low. Her masters had complete authority over her, and she was dependent on them for everything she needed to live. Hagar was from Egypt, so when she joined Abram's household, she left behind her homeland and culture, and possibly most if not all her family and friends as well.

Sarai's plan to make Hagar have a baby for her was not an uncommon thing in those times. The idea was that the servant was supposed to have children for a wife who was unable to get pregnant. The baby would be considered the wife's child and would be the master's heir. People believed that masters even owned their servants' bodies and could tell them what to do in every aspect of their lives.

When Hagar became pregnant, she began to act like she was more important than Sarai. It's possible Hagar believed that Abram would be so happy she was giving him the child he'd wanted for so long that he would make Hagar his chief wife, giving her a higher status than Sarai. But whatever the reason, Sarai was furious at Hagar's behavior, and Abram told her to do whatever she wanted to her servant. The Bible tells us that Sarai treated Hagar harshly. We don't know exactly what that means, but it was bad enough that Hagar was willing to risk running away. People usually traveled in groups in those days, and it would have been especially dangerous for a woman to be alone. Hagar was so miserable, she was willing to risk her and her baby's life to get away from Sarai.

→»»| HER GOD |«««-

The Bible tells us that God is not impressed when we act like some people are more important than others (see Galatians 3:28). We see that clearly in Hagar's story, where God gives a frightened, abused servant girl the same promise he gave to her wealthy, important boss. Since Abram gave Hagar's son the name God chose for him—Ishmael, which means "God hears"—we can assume Hagar told Abram about what happened to her. Ishmael's name would have been a lesson and a constant reminder to Abram and Sarai that God cared about Hagar.

Do you ever feel that no one really sees or hears you? Sometimes the world can be full of messages telling us we're less important or significant or loved than other people. Maybe you're the youngest in your family and it feels like your siblings or parents are too busy to really listen to you. Maybe it feels like everyone at school is more popular or better looking or has nicer things or is smarter or more athletic or more talented. Maybe you have a different skin color or ethnicity or culture than most of the people around you and it feels like no one truly understands or values you.

However small and unimportant and unnoticed you may feel, you can know for sure that God sees you. He sees every tear you cry in the dark (see Psalm 56:8); he knows all the things you secretly wish for. He loves you deeply and wants to be close to you. The God who saw a frightened servant girl in the middle of the desert is the same God who sees you today.

READ ABOUT HAGAR IN GENESIS 16; 21:9–21.

8

SARAH

STRONG IN HOPE

*It was by faith that even Sarah was able to have a child,
though she was barren and was too old. She believed that
God would keep his promise.*

HEBREWS 11:11, NLT

HER STORY

Sarah sat at the entrance of her tent, dusting flour off her hands. Her tired joints creaked so loudly that she thought her husband's surprise guests might hear them all the way under the tree where they sat eating the meal she'd hastily prepared. Sarah's husband, Abraham, stood near the three men, pouring fresh milk into their cups, passing them meat and bread and yogurt. Sarah had no idea where the men had come from or why they'd chosen to visit Abraham's camp today, but it was clear from the way her husband was acting that he thought they were important. He'd greeted them by bowing down to the ground, then dashed back to the tent. "Quick!" he'd gasped to Sarah. "Take some of your best flour and make bread!" Then he'd rushed off, servants running after him, to prepare the rest of the meal.

Fanning her sweaty brow with a hand, Sarah stretched out her aching legs. She was getting too old for hurried baking and surprise company. Sometimes it felt like she was getting too old for anything. There had been a time when life had felt full of hope and she'd believed that she and Abraham were destined for greatness, when the things he whispered to her in their tent at night—the promises God had made to him, to both of them, of more descendants than the stars—seemed to fill the whole world with joyful laughter. God had even changed their names from Abram and Sarai as a

symbol of the special relationship they had with him. But many, many years had passed with no signs of God's promises coming true, and now Sarah felt like if the world laughed, it was because it was making fun of her.

". . . Sarah, your wife?" Sarah sat up straight and leaned toward the tent's entrance. One of the strangers had said her name! She held her breath, straining to hear.

"She's there, inside the tent," Abraham said.

"I will come back and see you again this time next year," the stranger said. His voice wasn't loud, but it carried clearly to Sarah's ears. It seemed like even the birds and insects had fallen silent to listen. "When I come back," the stranger continued, "Sarah will have a son!"

She gasped. Month after month of her life had come and gone with no sign of a pregnancy. Sarah had counted wrinkle after wrinkle, gray hair after gray hair. Parts of her body that used to be full and firm and flexible had gotten baggy and soft and stiff.

She'd kept the faith for years, believing God's promise for Abraham's sake when she couldn't for her own. Fifteen years ago, she'd thought she'd had the answer when she'd given her slave Hagar to Abraham as a servant-wife and their son, Ishmael, had been born. She'd thought she could raise Ishmael as her own and build a family that way. But that plan had turned out to be a disaster. And Abraham kept insisting that God still meant for her, Sarah, to have a son of her own.

Now a stranger was sitting under their tree saying the same thing. Speaking as if with God's very own mouth. Promising she'd be pregnant within just a few months. Did she dare to hope again?

The midday sun beat down, shimmering on the desert dust. The jagged rocks and stunted trees seemed to be mocking Sarah. *This land is barren*, the birds seemed to squawk. *Just like you.* Long years of shame and disappointment welled up in Sarah's throat and escaped in a sarcastic huff of laughter. *The joy of a child isn't for a worn-out old bag like me, or an old man like my husband*, she thought. *I won't be made a fool of again.*

"What?" The amazement in the stranger's voice interrupted Sarah's bitter thoughts. An incredulous chuckle ran through his words. "Why did

Sarah laugh? Why did she say to herself, 'Can an old woman like me have a baby?' Is anything too hard for the Lord?"

Sarah's heart pounded. Who was this man, who spoke for God and read her secret thoughts? Fear clawed at her stomach. "I didn't laugh." She forced the words through dry lips.

"You did laugh." The stranger laid her lie bare, but strangely, Sarah no longer felt afraid. She felt seen and known and loved. And for the first time in many, many years, she felt something begin to grow in her heart, like a tiny green shoot uncurling in the midst of the desert. It felt like hope.

HER WORLD

Sarah was wealthy and beautiful. She had a husband who loved, valued, and respected her. But there was something big missing in her life—a child.

In Sarah's world, women who couldn't have babies not only felt sad about it but also often felt ashamed, like something was wrong with them or they had failed in some way. Some people believed that infertility was a sign that God was punishing you or at least didn't like you as much as other people.

Sarah got so desperate to get rid of her grief and embarrassment that she made Hagar become her husband's servant-wife so she could have a baby "for" Sarah. We know that by this time God had promised Abraham he would have lots of descendants and Abraham and Sarah had been waiting many years to have children. Maybe Sarah got tired of waiting, or maybe she thought she was helping God out by coming up with a practical solution to her and her husband's problem. But the Bible clearly tells us this was not what God had in mind, and it caused a lot of pain to everyone involved.

The arrival of the three strangers for a meal in Abraham's camp was a turning point in Sarah's life. In Bible times, eating together was an important part of making a covenant, or special agreement. God had made a covenant with Abraham in which he promised Sarah would have her own son. It was time for God to fulfill his promise, so he came in the form of those three travelers to have a covenant meal with Abraham. God included Sarah in his conversation with Abraham just as he had included her in the promise.

HER GOD

If you read the Bible, it won't take long for you to notice that God makes a habit of doing the unexpected, accomplishing the impossible, and bringing hope when all hope seems lost. We can see this clearly in God's choosing of Sarah, an infertile woman, to be the mother of his special people of promise. Perhaps God did that to show us that he is in control. As he told Sarah when she laughed in her tent, "Is anything too hard for the Lord?"

Have you ever wanted something really, really badly, but it seemed like it was never going to happen? We see those feelings in Sarah when she laughed at the idea God would give her a son in her old age. By this time, she had probably heard about Abraham's conversations with God—and God's promises—over and over. She had waited for years and years for them to come true, and now she was past the point when a woman's body is able to get pregnant. She had likely endured hearing the people around her gossip and whisper, wondering what was wrong with her that God wouldn't bless her with a child. And now a stranger was saying she would be pregnant in just a few months! Sarah was probably afraid to believe; she would rather mock the promise than be mocked again.

But the God of hope didn't let Sarah stay in a place of despair. He gently reminded her that nothing is impossible for God, and that he loves his people deeply and is always working for their good. Sarah's bitter chuckle turned to real laughter of joy when God gave her a baby boy, Isaac. We can imagine that all the years of sorrow and shame melted away when Sarah held her son in her arms for the first time. And we can share in her joy, because many generations later, God gave *us* a baby boy to take away our sorrow and shame—his Son, our Savior: Jesus.

> READ ABOUT SARAH IN GENESIS 11:29–31; 12:5, 10–20; 16; 17:15–21; 18:1–15; 20; 21:1–21; 23.

REBEKAH

STRONG IN FAITHFULNESS

They called Rebekah and asked her, "Will you go with this man?" "I will go," she said. . . . Isaac brought her into the tent of his mother Sarah, and he married Rebekah. So she became his wife, and he loved her; and Isaac was comforted after his mother's death.

GENESIS 24:58, 67

⇥⟫⟫| HER STORY |⟪⟪⟨

Rebekah admired the rose-gold sky as she made her way to the well outside town, expertly balancing her water jug on her shoulder. She smiled and waved to her friends and neighbors, pausing now and then to share a greeting, some news, or a funny story from her day. A cool breeze blew as the sun sank, a welcome change from the heat of the day.

It seemed unusually quiet as Rebekah got close to the well. The women often lingered for a few moments after they filled their jugs, visiting with friends before returning home to evening chores, but today the usual chatter was softer, a buzz of whispers. A stranger stood near the well, ten camels waiting behind him. Rebekah stared. Camels were rare and expensive. The stranger was well dressed, but his clothes didn't look like those of a man rich enough to own ten camels. He was probably the trusted servant of an extremely wealthy man.

The stranger looked intently at the women drawing water as if he were searching for someone. Could he be a friend or relative of one of Rebekah's neighbors? Who among her friends might be connected to such a person?

And why would he be looking for her at the well instead of going to her home and greeting her parents?

Rebekah walked to the well, stealing glances at the stranger from the corner of her eye. The camels groaned and growled, making some of the women jump. Rebekah looked over at the man again—he was looking back at her! She quickly looked away, her cheeks heating. What could the stranger want with her?

Rebekah filled her jug and turned toward home. Suddenly, she heard footsteps behind her and whirled around, heart pounding. The stranger was standing right in front of her. She could hear the whispers of the other women all around her.

"May I please have some water from your jug?" the man asked.

As strange as the situation was, Rebekah had been taught that it was important to be generous to strangers. "Of course, sir," she said, lowering the jug from her shoulder and holding it out to him. "Have as much as you'd like."

The man gulped water eagerly. His clothes and sandals were coated in dust. He must have come a long way. Rebekah peered at the camels. Some of them stood, heads drooping, while others had knelt, their long necks stretched out along the ground. She knew camels could drink a lot of water, many times what her jug could hold, but the poor animals looked so thirsty. She turned back to the man. "I'll get water for your camels too."

She dumped what was left in her jug into a water trough nearby and ran back to the well to refill it. She poured the water into the trough and went back to the well again. The camels crowded around, greedily sucking at the water, then raising their heads and shaking water droplets all over each other and Rebekah. It took many, many, many trips back and forth from the well to the trough before all the camels had drunk their fill. The sun was barely visible above the horizon and most of the other women had already gone home. Rebekah's parents and brothers would be wondering what was taking her so long. Her whole body was trembling with exhaustion, and she was damp and covered with dust and camel hair. She dragged herself back to the well one last time to get water to take home.

She turned from the well, wearily lifting the jug to her shoulder, to find the stranger standing near her again, a wide smile on his face and gold gleaming in his hands. He thanked her and handed her the jewelry—two bracelets and a nose ring, finer than anything she'd ever owned. His master was surely very rich for him to give such an expensive gift as thanks for a few jars of water! She slipped the bracelets onto her wrists and fastened the ring in her nose, glancing down at the jug to try to catch a glimpse of her reflection in the water. The stranger gave her a fatherly smile. "Who are your parents?" he asked. "And might you have room for a guest?"

"My father is Bethuel, the son of Nahor and Milcah," she answered. "And yes, we have plenty of room. I will go and tell my family you are here."

Rebekah raced home, the gold heavy and unfamiliar on her wrists and nose. Her brother, Laban, took one look at the jewelry and barely waited to hear what Rebekah had to say before racing to bring the wealthy stranger back to the house. Rebekah's family prepared a feast for their guest, but before he ate he insisted on telling them about his mission to find a wife for his master's son. The family was amazed to hear that the man's master was Abraham, Rebekah's great-uncle!

"God has shown unfailing love and faithfulness to my master all his life," the servant said. "He has given him great wealth and a son in his old age. And God has shown his faithfulness again today by leading me straight to Abraham's family to find a wife for his son, Isaac. Will you also show unfailing love and faithfulness to your relative by allowing me to take Rebekah to be Isaac's wife?"

Rebekah caught her breath. Was she willing to leave behind everyone and everything she'd ever known to marry a stranger? But she couldn't stop thinking about this God her great-uncle had left his family and home and gods to follow, a faithful God who didn't go back on his promises and cared for humans like they were his own children.

"It's obvious God has led you here," Rebekah's father said to the man. Her brother nodded. "Rebekah should be Isaac's wife." Abraham's servant bowed down to the ground and thanked his God. He gave Rebekah and her family even more expensive gifts, and then they finally ate.

When the family woke up the next day, Abraham's servant had already been busy for a long time, getting ready to go. Her brother and mother asked him to stay longer, but the man was determined to leave right away. So they called Rebekah and asked, "Are you willing to go with this man now?"

Rebekah looked at her mother and brother and at all the familiar objects in her home. She looked at the stranger who was waiting for her to decide whether she would leave all of it behind forever—right now.

"I will go," she replied. She would show faithful love to her relatives and to her future husband. And deep in her heart, she hoped and believed that their God would show his faithful love to her too.

→»»| HER WORLD |««←

Have you been to a wedding or even been part of a wedding party? Many of the weddings we attend today are big, fancy occasions that are planned by the bride and groom for months or even years. Many brides and grooms today want to start their marriage with a memorable celebration that reflects their personalities or other things that are important to them.

Things were quite different in Bible times. While in many cultures today who and when to marry is up to the couple, in Rebekah's culture it was more of a family decision. As we read in Genesis 24, Abraham, as Isaac's father, was the one to decide that it was time for his son to get married, and he told his servant where his son's bride should come from. And the servant asks Rebekah's parents and brother if they will agree to the marriage (though we do see Rebekah's family asking her opinion, which tells us young women at the time likely did get some say).

Wedding ceremonies were also very different—that is, we don't see the Bible describe many ceremonies at all! There's no mention of a minister or rabbi or judge or anyone else officiating the ceremony. Once the two families had agreed to the marriage, the bride and groom were considered a couple and started their life together. Gifts would be exchanged, as we see in this story, and sometimes there was a family party, though Rebekah and Isaac don't seem to even have had that. At the end of Genesis 24, Rebekah and Isaac meet, and Isaac brings her into his mother's tent—and they were married, just like that! (Though, interestingly, this story does mention a tradition that we still see in many weddings today: the bridal veil. See Genesis 24:65).

➤➤➤ | HER GOD | ◄◄◄

This is the longest chapter in Genesis, and its main theme is God's love for his people. The Hebrew word used to describe this love, *chesed*, is translated into English in different ways—"faithful love," "loyal love," "unfailing love," "steadfast love." It's a love that never quits, no matter what. God's faithful love is mentioned over and over in the Bible (see Psalm 118 for an entire song about it). It's God's most essential and most important characteristic; in fact, the Bible tells us, "God *is* love" (1 John 4:8, emphasis added).

Rebekah seems to have been so drawn to the story of God's faithful love that she was willing to leave everything she knew and loved far behind to show faithful love to relatives she'd never met. God rewarded her faithfulness by including her in his family, his people of promise. She became one of the ancestors of Jesus, the ultimate expression of God's faithful love!

READ ABOUT REBEKAH IN GENESIS 24; 25:19–27; 26:7–11; 27.

LEAH

STRONG LOVE

When the Lord saw that Leah was not loved, he enabled
her to conceive, but Rachel remained childless. . . . [Leah]
conceived again, and when she gave birth to a son she said,
"This time I will praise the Lord." So she named him Judah.

GENESIS 29:31, 35

→»»| HER STORY |«««-

Leah cradled her newborn son in her arms and kissed his downy head. This was the fourth time she'd held one of her babies right after his birth, but she felt just as much wonder and amazement as the first time. Maybe even more. When this little boy's brothers were born, she'd been so anxious for their father—her husband, Jacob—to show that he loved them and approved of them—and of her—that she'd almost forgotten to pay attention to how miraculous they were.

Leah's maid, Zilpah, slipped into the room. "Your older sons want to see you and the baby," she said. "Should I tell them to wait until Jacob has visited?"

Leah smiled. "No," she said. "Jacob will come when he comes. Tell my sons they can meet their new brother."

Her older sons—Reuben, Simeon, and Levi—tiptoed into the room, eyes wide. Leah held out her free arm to them and gathered them close. "This is your baby brother," she said. "Isn't he wonderful?"

The boys peered at the baby. Reuben reached out a finger and gently touched his cheek. "What is his name, Mother?"

Leah looked at her oldest son, remembering his birth. The name

Reuben meant "Look, a son!" How she'd hoped that Jacob would love her for giving him his first son! She knew he would never love her as much as he loved Rachel, his other wife and Leah's younger sister. Leah had never been able to compete with Rachel in anything. Definitely not in looks—everyone had always talked about Rachel's beauty, ever since they were little. Men always noticed Rachel. Jacob had fallen in love with her practically the instant he'd arrived in their town. Leah and Rachel's father, Laban, had only cared about how much money he could get for his daughters by marrying them off. He'd tricked Jacob into marrying Leah first and then given him Rachel as a second wife. Jacob had never made any secret of the fact that Rachel was his favorite.

But Leah had won in one thing—she had now given Jacob four sons, while Rachel hadn't gotten pregnant even once. Leah knew this made her sister sick with jealousy, and their rivalry had become so intense that they were almost enemies now. Deep in her heart, Leah had felt a tiny bit of sadness for her sister's pain, but she'd mostly felt sick and tired of being second best, the one nobody wanted or cared about. She would have done anything for Jacob's love. She'd tried to tell him that through their sons' names—she'd named her second son Simeon, which meant "one who hears," telling anyone who would listen, "The Lord heard that I was unloved and has given me another son." Jacob hadn't gotten the hint that time either, so when their third son was born, she'd called him Levi—"being attached"—thinking that surely Jacob would feel attachment or affection for her after she'd given him three sons. But he hadn't.

But now, looking at this fourth beautiful, miraculous baby boy, and his older brothers cuddling close to her, Leah knew that someone had loved her the whole time. She'd known it for a long time, really, but she'd been so focused on gaining Jacob's love that she hadn't paid attention. God had shown her love. He had seen she was rejected, forgotten, second best. And he'd allowed her to be the one who gave Jacob children, instead of Rachel. Jacob hadn't been able to push Leah aside completely because she was the mother of his sons. Amazingly, it seemed that God cared about a plain, sad girl enough to watch over her and give her these four beautiful gifts.

Leah smiled at Reuben, Simeon, and Levi. "I will name the baby Judah," she told them. "It means praise—because this time, I am praising the Lord."

→»»| HER WORLD |«««-

In Leah's time and culture, when a man wanted to marry a woman, he would offer her father money, property, or some other valuable thing to show respect for the woman's family and how much he wanted to marry her. Jacob (the son of Rebekah from the previous story) offered Leah's father, Laban (Rebekah's brother and Jacob's uncle), seven years of free work in order to marry Leah's sister, Rachel. That was a very valuable offer. We know from the Bible that Laban was a greedy person and didn't mind cheating people to get what he wanted. It's likely Laban figured that Leah wouldn't get as good a marriage proposal, since she wasn't as beautiful as Rachel. So when it was time for Rachel to put on her bridal veil and go into Jacob's tent to become his wife, Laban sent Leah instead. When Jacob confronted Laban about his trickery, Laban got Jacob to agree to give him seven *more* years of work so he could marry Rachel too.

It was common in this time and culture for a man to have more than one wife. Often one wife would have more status or importance than the others. Rachel would have had an advantage over Leah because Jacob loved her more. But God gave Leah importance by allowing her to have children while Rachel was unable to get pregnant. As we've already seen, children were considered a sign of God's favor.

→»»| HER GOD |«««-

Have you ever felt less than or second best? Like you can't even compete, so you might as well not bother? Leah had probably felt that way her entire life. The Bible says "Leah had weak eyes, but Rachel had a lovely figure and was beautiful" (Genesis 29:17). (The phrase "weak eyes" is translated in several different ways in different versions of the Bible because translators aren't sure exactly what it means in the original language, Hebrew. But it's clear the Bible is saying Leah couldn't touch Rachel when it came to looks.) Rachel got more attention and was considered more valuable because she was physically beautiful. Does that sound familiar? Some things definitely haven't changed since Bible times!

But God makes it clear he doesn't see people that way. In fact, we see over and over in the Bible that God pays special attention to people the world considers less valuable. He showed special love to Leah, who was rejected and unloved by the people who should have cared for her most. And we see evidence that Leah reflected God's love to others later in her life. Rachel eventually had two sons, but she died young. In later years, Jacob refers to Leah as the "mother" of one of Rachel's sons, Joseph (see Genesis 37:10). Perhaps Leah was able to set aside her rivalry with her sister and show love to Rachel's sons after she died. But we know for sure that she praised God for seeing and loving her when she was unloved, just as he had with Hagar many years before. And Leah's son Judah, whose name means "praise," was one of the ancestors of Jesus, God himself who came to earth to love the unloved and forgotten.

> READ ABOUT LEAH IN GENESIS 29; 30; 37:10; 49:31.

RACHEL

IN GOD'S STRONG HANDS

*God remembered Rachel; he listened to her and enabled
her to conceive. She became pregnant and gave birth to a
son and said, "God has taken away my disgrace."*

GENESIS 30:22-23

HER STORY

Rachel patted her baby boy's back as she watched the sons her servant had
given her, Dan and Naphtali, play with their brothers. Rachel sighed, her
arms and legs heavy with exhaustion. She didn't feel tired only because
baby Joseph woke her up several times a night. She was worn out from her
years-long battle with her sister over their husband's love.

Rachel had been furious when her father stole what should have been
her wedding and her husband and handed them to Leah. Even though
Jacob loved her best, she hated having to share him. And her anger had
grown as Leah gave birth to son after son—Reuben, Simeon, Levi, Judah—
while Rachel watched month after month slip away with no baby of her
own. Finally, she had given her maid Bilhah to Jacob as a servant-wife, and
Dan and Naphtali were born. Rachel had thought she was finally winning.
But then Leah had given Jacob *her* servant, Zilpah, who gave her Gad and
Asher.

Then Rachel had tried eating mandrakes, a plant that was supposed to
help women have babies. But that hadn't worked either. Leah had gotten
pregnant instead! She'd had two more sons and a daughter, while Rachel
waited and waited, furious and miserable.

Then, finally, when Rachel had almost given up hope, Joseph had

come. She could still hardly believe that the years of feeling ashamed, of pretending she didn't hear her neighbors and relatives whisper and gossip about her, of watching Leah parade around with baby after baby, were over. For years she'd dreamed of this moment. She thought she'd feel triumph. She'd imagined how good it would feel to brag to Leah that she had Jacob's love *and* a son.

But all Rachel felt was tired. Nothing she'd tried to give herself children had worked. For years God had kept her from having children, and now he had given her a son. Why? She had no idea. She was just grateful God had taken away her shame and given her the beautiful little boy in her arms.

Rachel looked across to where Leah sat, her little daughter, Dinah, in her lap. She wondered if Leah was tired too. Maybe things could be different between them now.

→»»| HER WORLD |««←

We know that Jacob was in love with Rachel—so much that he was willing to work fourteen years without pay to marry her—but the Bible doesn't tell us how Rachel felt about Jacob. In Rachel's time, young women didn't have a lot of say in who or when they married. Their father or other male relatives made that decision. Perhaps some fathers thought about their daughters' feelings when they were choosing husbands for them, but that doesn't seem to be the case with Rachel and Leah's father, Laban. He was only interested in how much wealth he could get out of their marriages. (He continued to take advantage of Jacob until finally Jacob, Leah, Rachel, and their family ran away from him.)

Sadly, just as Rachel and Leah's father didn't do a good job caring for them, they didn't do a very good job caring for each other. Instead of being friends and allies, they became enemies, always competing, always jealous of each other. Rachel had Jacob's love but wanted children. Leah had children but wanted Jacob's love. Instead of sticking together and being grateful for what they had, they each made themselves miserable wishing for what the other had. They tried to one-up each other instead of supporting one another. And their rivalry affected other people as well. Like Sarah did with Hagar, the sisters used their servants to have children for them, taking those babies as their own.

-»»| HER GOD |«««-

Rachel made herself and the people around her miserable because she was desperate to control her ability to bear children, but that was God's future to decide. She became a jealous rival to her sister, hurt her relationship with her husband with her constant complaining and blaming, and treated her servant like a tool to get what she wanted.

When Joseph was finally born, Rachel seems to have realized the truth. Nothing she did to have children worked. Only God was able to give her that. We don't know for sure, but it's possible Rachel and Leah were able to have a better relationship after Joseph's birth. The Bible doesn't mention more conflict between them, and we actually see them agreeing in one of the last stories where they appear together (see Genesis 31:4–16).

What we can know for sure is that we can trust God to be in charge of our lives and our world. We won't always understand why he does what he does or allows certain things to happen and not others. Some things he brings our way probably won't seem good at the time. Even Jesus, God's perfect Son, asked his Father to do things differently (see Matthew 26:36–42). But he trusted that God knew best. With his help and strength, we can do the same.

> READ ABOUT RACHEL IN GENESIS 29; 30; 31; 33:1–2, 7; 35:16–26; 46:19, 22, 25; 48:7.

SHIPHRAH AND PUAH

STRENGTH TO RESIST

The midwives, however, feared God and did not do what the king of Egypt had told them to do. . . . So God was kind to the midwives.

EXODUS 1:17, 20

THEIR STORY

Puah nervously glanced at her friend Shiphrah as they stood outside the pharaoh's throne room. Neither had dreamed they would find themselves in the king's presence—they were simply enslaved women who, as midwives, helped their fellow enslaved women have their babies. But because those women included Hebrews—said to be God's special people, part of his promise—here they were for the second time, waiting to speak to the man who had everything they didn't—freedom, wealth, power. The power to kill them for what they were about to say.

Shiphrah caught Puah's eye. "Have courage," she whispered. "Follow my lead." Puah nodded, swallowing hard. Then an official beckoned them to come forward and bow before the pharaoh.

The king of Egypt scowled at them. "Not long ago," he said, glaring from one woman to the other, "the two of you stood before me in this very room, and I gave you an order. Didn't I?"

"Yes, Your Majesty," Shiphrah and Puah whispered. Puah knew she would never forget that day, no matter how much she wished she could. She had felt chills run up and down her body at the king's terrible words: "When you help the Hebrew women as they give birth, watch as they deliver. If the baby is a boy, kill him; if it is a girl, let her live." The two midwives had known

their lives would be in danger if they dared to disobey the pharaoh. But they served a greater King, one who would never want them to harm innocent babies. So Shiphrah and Puah had prayed for courage and then chosen to obey God over the pharaoh. They knew the Egyptian king would eventually find out they were not following his evil orders. And that day had come.

Puah kept her eyes on the floor, afraid to look at the pharaoh's face. "Why have you disobeyed me?" the ruler demanded. "Why have you allowed the Hebrew boys to live?"

Puah heard Shiphrah take a deep breath. "Hebrew women aren't like Egyptian women, Your Majesty," she said. "They have their babies so quickly that we can't get there in time to do anything." Puah nodded along, peeking up at the pharaoh to see how he was taking Shiphrah's answer.

The Egyptian king scowled even harder. He was quiet a long time. Puah barely dared to breathe.

"Obviously, I can't count on you to help me," he finally growled. "I will have to think of another plan. I should have known better than to rely on slave women." He waved his hand impatiently. "Get out of my sight!"

Puah and Shiphrah nearly ran from the throne room, not slowing down until they got to Shiphrah's house, far from the palace. Their knees suddenly felt weak and they almost collapsed to the floor.

"What do you think the pharaoh will do now?" Puah asked her friend.

Shiphrah shook her head. "I don't know," she said. "I fear he will not give up his plan to destroy our people." She reached over and squeezed Puah's hand. "But by God's grace, he will not use us to do it."

⇢⟫⟫⟩| THEIR WORLD |⟨⟨⟨⟵

This story takes place hundreds of years after the time of Leah and Rachel. By Shiphrah and Puah's time, the Hebrews had been enslaved by the Egyptians and were forced to make bricks and build buildings for them. But even though their lives were very hard, God blessed them with children and their population grew. The pharaoh of this story became very worried that the Hebrews would join with his enemies and become a threat to his land and people. So he came up with his horrible plan and tried to force Shiphrah and Puah to do his dirty work.

Since there were so many Israelites, they likely weren't the only midwives helping deliver their babies. It's possible they supervised the other midwives, or they are named in this story as representatives of all the midwives. Some people who study the Bible believe Shiphrah and Puah were Egyptian, which could explain why the pharaoh thought they might help with his plan. But their names are Hebrew, so it seems likely they were Israelites the pharaoh thought he could bully because he was king and they were enslaved. Either way, they chose to obey God rather than the pharaoh, and God rewarded them for that.

THEIR GOD

God tells us in the Bible that he wants us to respect and obey people who are in authority over us (see Romans 13:1). But the Bible also tells about times when human rules clearly went against God's laws. Shiphrah and Puah knew it was wrong to obey the pharaoh's command to kill the baby Hebrew boys because only God has the right to give and take life. It was certainly not easy for the two women to go against the pharaoh's orders. He easily could have punished them severely or even had them killed. But God gave the midwives courage and strength to resist the pharaoh's evil laws.

Even today we may encounter a rule or law that is truly unfair or wrong. Some rules are meant to give advantage to one group of people over another, which goes against God's teaching that all people are made in his image and have equal worth in his eyes. Or sometimes a person in authority might ask us to do something we know is wrong. If that happens, we can be confident that God will give us the same strength and courage he gave to Shiphrah and Puah.

READ ABOUT SHIPHRAH AND PUAH IN EXODUS 1:15–21.

When [Jochebed] could hide [her baby] no longer, she got a papyrus basket for him and coated it with tar and pitch. Then she placed the child in it and put it among the reeds along the bank of the Nile.

EXODUS 2:3

→»»| HER STORY |«««←

Jochebed finished feeding her baby boy and wrapped him up snugly. He started to fuss, and she swayed back and forth to soothe him, movements that had become familiar in the three months since he'd been born—the three months she'd been hiding him from the Egyptians. All day and all night, she'd been alert for the tiniest cry, watching the baby's face for signs that he was upset and swooping in to quiet him as quickly as she could. Even when she was deeply asleep, exhausted from a long day of working and caring for this baby and her two older children, she sprang awake at the slightest sound. The baby's life depended on it. If any Egyptian learned a baby boy lived in this house, they would come and take him away, throwing him into the Nile River as they had with so many others.

But she couldn't continue like this. Hiding a baby had never been easy, but it got harder every day, as the tiny boy grew and became more active and aware. He was no longer content to sleep most of the day in a basket. Soon, he would be able to move around on his own. Jochebed had prayed and cried, and cried and prayed, and now she had a plan. She wasn't sure it was a good plan—in fact, she was often convinced it was a terrible idea,

as so many things could go wrong—but she knew there was nothing else she could do for her baby. She would have to trust God would take care of him now.

The baby was fast asleep. Jochebed placed him in the special basket she had been working on for days. It was woven of papyrus reeds, and she had coated it with tar and pitch so it would be waterproof. She made sure the baby's blanket was tucked tightly around him and took a last, long look at his precious, sleeping face. With a deep breath, she said a silent, desperate prayer. *Please save him. Please, let this not be the last time I see his face.*

She had to move quickly, while he was still asleep. She settled the lid on the basket and turned to see her daughter peeking through the doorway, eyes wide. She beckoned to her. "Come with me, Miriam. Quick!"

Carefully carrying the basket between them, Jochebed and Miriam hurried through alleys and behind their neighbors' houses, making their way to the Nile as quickly and quietly as they could. Jochebed whispered prayers the whole time. Finally, they reached the river.

Jochebed lifted the basket's lid for one last look. The baby was still sleeping peacefully. Miriam gently brushed his cheek with her finger. She looked up at her mother, her face puzzled and questioning.

Jochebed couldn't pause to answer her daughter's questions or think about her own fears. If she didn't act now, she would lose her nerve—and any chance her baby might have at a life. She set the basket in the water and gave it a gentle push. It began to drift downstream.

"Mother!" Miriam gasped. Jochebed grabbed her arm.

"Miriam, listen! Stand by the bank and keep your eyes on that basket. Watch and see what happens to your baby brother." A young girl hanging around the riverbank would be less obvious than a grown woman. Plus, Jochebed needed to get back to her work before anyone noticed she was missing. She gave Miriam a quick kiss, glanced one more time at the little basket with its precious cargo, took a final deep breath, and turned toward home. Her arms felt so empty without her baby in them. But she had put him into the safest arms of all. God was holding him now.

HER WORLD

After the midwives refused to help the pharaoh, he ordered the Egyptians to throw any baby Hebrew boys they found into the Nile River. When Jochebed had her baby boy, she hid him for as long as she could, but it was only a matter of time before someone found him. It's interesting that Jochebed took her baby to the place where so many other babies had been killed in order to save him. Some people who study the Bible believe she took him to a particular spot in the river on purpose, hoping a certain person would find him (keep reading to find out who that person was!).

First with the midwives and then with the order to throw babies into the river, the pharaoh allowed baby Hebrew girls to live. Why? Some people think the pharaoh didn't want to lose too many slaves. If he killed all the Hebrew babies, eventually the parents would grow old and die, and there would be no more Hebrews. But if he let the girls live, he could make them marry men from another enslaved group. They would also become part of that group and lose their Israelite culture.

Another possibility is that the pharaoh simply didn't see girls and women as a threat and couldn't be bothered to deal with them. Like many people throughout history, the pharaoh believed women and girls were not as important or strong as men and boys. But God does not agree! He used the women the pharaoh ignored to bring about what the king feared the most.

HER GOD

Next time you get a chance, ask your mom or another mother you know how they would have felt about setting their three-month-old baby afloat in a basket on one of the world's longest rivers. Jochebed showed incredible trust in God!

How was she able to show that kind of faith? She knew God cares for and loves his people even more than a good mother cares for and loves her child (see Isaiah 46:3–4; 49:13–16). She knew only God could save her son, just as only God could save her enslaved people.

Why did God save Jochebed's baby and not the babies who were thrown into the river? For that matter, why did God not stop his special people from being enslaved in the first place? We don't know the answers to those questions—or to many other hard questions we may ask about all the bad things that happen in our world. But we can know that God is still good and trustworthy and that he still loves us, no matter what (see Matthew 10:29–31). Our world is broken, and many evil things happen. But in the end, good will win, and God's love will make all things new.

READ ABOUT JOCHEBED IN EXODUS 2:1–10; 6:20.

MIRIAM

A STRONG GUARDIAN

[The baby's] sister stood at a distance to see what would happen to him.

EXODUS 2:4

⟶ HER STORY ⟵

Miriam stood by the Nile River bank, watching her mother hurry away. She locked her hands together, trying to stop the shaking. Her mother glanced back, eyes flitting from Miriam's face to the basket in the river.

The basket! Remembering her mission, Miriam turned back to the Nile. The waterproofed basket was still there, bobbing gently among the papyrus reeds by the shore. Miriam found an especially thick and tall clump of reeds and crouched behind it, mud squelching under her feet.

Miriam strained her ears, but the only sound she heard was the river, lapping against the shore. She hoped her baby brother was still asleep, snug and dry inside his floating bed. How long was she supposed to stay and watch? What should she do if the basket started to sink? Or if a crocodile got too close? What if an Egyptian got curious and fished the basket out of the river? It wouldn't take them long to figure out her brother was a Hebrew boy if they looked closely at him. Then what?

Miriam remembered her mother's whispered prayers as they took the basket to the river. Many times, as she had listened to others pray, Miriam had wondered if anyone was listening. Her people had been praying for deliverance for hundreds of years. If God was really listening, it was taking him a long time to answer. And even if he was listening, did he care about the prayers of one young girl watching over one tiny baby?

The basket suddenly bobbed wildly on a passing wave, and Miriam decided to take her chances. *Please keep him safe,* she prayed. *And please help me know what to do, and give me the courage to do it.*

She'd barely finished her prayer when movement on the far shore caught her eye. A group was coming down to the river—young Egyptian women in clothes Miriam usually only saw in her dreams. The woman in the middle was dressed even more beautifully than her companions, outshining them like the sun outshines the stars. As they got close to the water, Miriam heard them talking. She gasped. This must be a princess—the pharaoh's daughter! What would she do if she saw the baby?

Miriam frantically looked from the basket to the women. Could she wade into the river and grab the basket without being seen? But then the princess called out to one of her ladies-in-waiting and pointed right at the basket! The servant began to wade toward it.

Miriam shrank into the reeds, heart pounding. What should she do?

Instantly, an unexplainable peace filled her heart, slowing her breath and quieting her trembling. Her mother had told her to watch. She would watch and trust, and pray.

The lady-in-waiting towed the basket over to the princess. The pharaoh's daughter lifted the lid, and the baby's cries drifted over the water toward Miriam. She held her breath and shielded her eyes with her hand, squinting at the princess.

The princess stared into the basket for a moment. Then Miriam watched her face soften. She could see her compassionate expression all the way across the river. The princess reached into the basket and picked the baby up, holding him a bit awkwardly but with tenderness.

Suddenly, Miriam knew what she was supposed to do next. She stood up, and waded into the river, toward the princess.

⟫⟫| HER WORLD |⟪⟪

This is one of the most well-known stories about Miriam in the Bible—but this portion of Scripture doesn't mention her by name! However, since she is the only daughter who appears in the Bible's lists of Jochebed's children (see Numbers 26:59; 1 Chronicles 6:3), most likely the sister mentioned in this story is indeed Miriam.

In Miriam's time and culture, women were almost always most known for being wives and mothers. So it's interesting that the Bible never mentions in later stories whether Miriam had a husband or children; instead, it tells us about the gifts and talents God gave her. When she grew up, Miriam became a prophet: a person who receives special messages from God and passes them on to his people. (Miriam is the first female prophet mentioned in the Bible.) The Bible also says that she praised God by singing, dancing, and playing instruments.

⟶⟫⟫| HER GOD |⟪⟪⟵

Miriam is one of the women God used to save his people from slavery in Egypt. We don't know how old she was when this story took place, but she was likely very young, still a girl living with her parents. In Miriam's world, it would have been hard to imagine a less important or powerful person than a young enslaved girl. But God chose her to watch over her brother and make sure he would survive the river and grow up safe and loved. Later, God chose her to be a respected leader among her people.

Do you ever feel small and unimportant? Like you're always being overlooked or fading into the background? No matter how low your status at school, on the team, or even in your family, you can know for sure you are important to God. He gave you your unique talents and characteristics on purpose, and he thinks you're amazing! He wants to be your friend. He wants to do good things through you—now, just as you are, right where you are. And he'll give you whatever you need to do them.

> READ ABOUT MIRIAM IN EXODUS 2:1–10;
> EXODUS 15:20–21; NUMBERS 12:1–15; 20:1.

PHARAOH'S DAUGHTER

STRONG IN COMPASSION

When the princess opened [the basket], she saw the baby. The little boy was crying, and she felt sorry for him.

EXODUS 2:6, NLT

HER STORY

The Egyptian princess swirled her hand through the water of the Nile River. The river was very important to her people—they even believed it had healing powers. Bathing in the river was a special part of the princess's day.

The princess's ladies-in-waiting paced along the riverbank, guarding her and ready to attend to any need or want she might have. Papyrus reeds waved and rustled in the wind as she enjoyed the cool water and the warm morning sunshine.

Soon, something caught the princess's eye. She peered at it, raising her hand to shield her eyes from the sun. What could it be?

"It looks like there's a basket caught in the reeds over there," the princess called to one of her ladies-in-waiting. "Go get it and bring it to me."

The servant hurried to obey, and soon the princess was lifting the cover off a basket woven from reeds. She gasped. There was a baby inside! Sunlight fell on the tiny boy's face, and he awoke. He looked up into the princess's eyes and started to cry.

"Poor little thing," murmured the princess. She looked closely at the baby. "This must be one of the Hebrew children." She knew her father, the pharaoh, felt the Hebrews were a threat to his kingdom and had ordered

43

all their newborn baby boys be killed. But the princess did not want this baby to die. It was like he had been placed in the reeds especially for her to find—a gift from the mighty and sacred Nile. She lifted the baby into her arms. "There, there," she whispered, holding him close. "I will keep you safe."

She could feel the curious gazes of her ladies-in-waiting, but she ignored them for now. She cuddled the tiny, soft body protectively close to her chest and gently rocked back and forth. The baby stopped crying and closed his eyes. The princess's heart filled with tenderness. She admired the baby's round cheeks and long eyelashes, until a soft cough behind her made her turn.

"Excuse me, Your Highness," one of her servants said. "A Hebrew girl wants to say something to you. Do you wish to speak to her?"

The princess looked over to where another of her ladies stood next to a young girl. What could she want? Interesting, too, that a Hebrew girl had shown up right after the Hebrew baby. "Yes, let her come to me."

The girl came forward and bowed. "Your Highness, would you like me to find one of the Hebrew women to nurse that baby for you?"

The princess smiled. Here was another gift from the Nile. Surely the girl coming to her with this offer was a sign she was meant to save this child. She would raise him to be a great man, one who would do mighty deeds. "Yes, please bring the nurse!" she said. The girl soon returned with a woman she introduced as her mother, Jochebed. The princess handed the boy to the Hebrew woman, who took him eagerly, feeling his little arms and legs as if checking he was safe and uninjured. The baby looked up into the woman's face and smiled. The princess smiled too. "Nurse this child for me. I will pay you for your help." Jochebed held the baby close, tears streaming down her face.

A few years later, Jochebed brought her little boy to live with the princess, who adopted him as her son. The princess named him Moses, and he grew up to be one of the greatest leaders of God's people, showing powerful signs from God and leading the Hebrews out of their slavery in Egypt.

HER WORLD

We can't be sure of this princess's name because Bible experts aren't certain which pharaoh reigned when Moses was born. There are a few popular ideas. Some believe the pharaoh was Rameses, who had many daughters. Historians have suggested the princess was named Tharmuth/Thermouthis or Merris.

Another interesting idea is that the pharaoh was named Thutmose I and the princess was his daughter Hatshepsut. Hatshepsut eventually became pharaoh herself, one of ancient Egypt's few female rulers, even though she wasn't allowed to inherit the throne from her father because she was a girl. Instead, she was married to her half brother, her father's son by one of his concubines (servant wives). Hatshepsut's only child was a girl, so when her husband died, her stepson became the official pharaoh. Since he was very young, Hatshepsut became regent, someone who handles the practical government of a country when the ruler can't. Eventually she named herself pharaoh, perhaps because the nation was under threat of attack and needed to show they had a powerful ruler on the throne.

Historians believe Hatshepsut had a very close relationship with her father and that she was a courageous woman who was willing to take bold risks to do what she believed was right. If she was the woman in the story, this could explain why the princess decided to go against her father's command and how she was able to get the royal family to accept a Hebrew boy as one of their own. But no matter which Egyptian princess was his adoptive mother, as a member of the pharaoh's household, Moses likely would have gotten military and government training, which would have prepared him to lead his people when he grew up.

The pharaoh believed that women and girls would not be strong enough to cause him any trouble, and that he could use them like tools to grow his population of slaves. But God gave the women of Exodus—Shiphrah, Puah, Jochebed, Miriam, and the pharaoh's own daughter—power, strength, and courage to fight against the ruler's unjust and cruel law and save the life of the child who would go on to lead God's people out of slavery.

HER GOD

Having compassion on someone means feeling what they are feeling and wanting to help them. God had compassion on his people in their slavery, so he sent Moses to help save them. He had compassion on Moses's birth mother, who couldn't keep her baby safe by herself, by allowing her to care for Moses while he was a baby. Even though Pharaoh's daughter probably worshiped false Egyptian gods, the true God used her to show his compassion to his people when she saved Moses's life and paid his mother to nurse him. We don't know for sure if the princess realized Jochebed was Moses's mother, but it's certainly possible! Either way, her actions suggest she saw these Hebrews as humans like her, even though her fellow Egyptians considered them lesser people they could enslave and kill. She reflected God in this too—all people are made in his image and are precious to him.

Some people think a compassionate and tender heart is a weakness, but God disagrees. When, years after this story, Moses asked God to show him his glory, God named himself "the God of compassion" (Exodus 34:6, NLT). In this story, God showed the princess's compassion was stronger than her father's cruelty. Centuries later, he showed the strongest compassion when he lived and died as a human to save his people from sin. And he continues to have compassion on us—on you!—today in many different ways. God is mighty in compassion!

READ ABOUT PHARAOH'S DAUGHTER IN EXODUS 2:1–10.

ZIPPORAH

STRENGTH TO CROSS BORDERS

Moses agreed to stay with [Reuel], who gave his daughter Zipporah to Moses in marriage.

EXODUS 2:21

→»»| HER STORY |««←

The first cool breeze of the evening was beginning to blow as Zipporah walked behind her father's flock with her six sisters, talking and laughing as they took the sheep to get water. Zipporah's shoulders and feet ached after a long day herding in the desert, and she was looking forward to sitting down for supper, telling her father and mother about the things she'd seen and thought that day, teasing her youngest sister, whispering with her oldest sister about their hopes and dreams for the future. Zipporah often wondered what the future held for her. Most likely she would marry a man like her father, an important person in their community, and live a comfortable life in Midian, the land where she had been born.

The sisters reached the well and started to draw water for their sheep. But suddenly rough shouts rang out across the desert. Zipporah wheeled around, gripping her staff. A group of shepherds ran up to the well, pushing through the sisters' flock. "Get away!" one of them yelled, waving a club in the air. "It's our turn!"

Another man barked an ugly laugh. "Run away, little girls," he sneered, shoving one of Zipporah's sisters. Zipporah clenched her teeth. She hated the idea of giving in to these rude and rough men. She and her sisters had arrived first; how dare these shepherds demand they move their entire flock away from the well without giving them water? She traded looks with her sisters.

She could tell they also wanted to take a stand, but it was too dangerous. There were too many men, and they looked ready to become violent.

"Hey!" A new voice called out, cutting across the shepherds' taunts. Zipporah turned to see an Egyptian man striding up, his chest out and head high like he was some prince.

"Stand aside," the stranger commanded. "And show respect. These women arrived first. Once they have given their sheep water, you can bring your flocks up."

"Who's going to make us?" the tallest shepherd demanded, scowling at the Egyptian.

"I am," the stranger replied. Zipporah had to admire his boldness— even though he was outnumbered, he acted like he expected to be obeyed without question. He folded his arms and stared the shepherds down.

The other men looked at the stranger, then looked at each other, now seeming uncertain. "Move," the Egyptian insisted. The shepherds grumbled but then slowly obeyed. Zipporah raised her eyebrows. One of her sisters giggled.

The stranger held his pose until all the shepherds had backed off, returning to their flocks some distance away. Then he relaxed and smiled at the sisters. "Let's get your sheep watered, shall we?" He quickly drew enough water for the entire flock. Zipporah and her sisters tried to help, but he insisted they sit and rest in the shade. Zipporah watched the man work, ignoring her sisters' whispers and snickers.

When all the sheep had been watered, the sisters thanked the stranger and hurried home. They rushed to tell their father, Reuel, what had happened at the well. "Wait, wait!" Reuel laughed. "Not all at once! Zipporah, you tell me." Zipporah quickly recounted how the stranger had saved the sisters from the rough shepherds and watered the flock for them.

"What?" Reuel exclaimed. "If this man did what you say, why on earth did you leave him there by the well? What were you thinking? This strong and generous stranger should be sitting at my table right now, sharing a meal with us. Go and get him! Go on, now!" He shooed his daughters back outside, laughing and shaking his head.

ZELOPHEHAD'S DAUGHTERS

STRENGTH TO CHANGE LAWS

The Lord said to [Moses], "What Zelophehad's daughters are saying is right. You must certainly give them property as an inheritance among their father's relatives and give their father's inheritance to them."

NUMBERS 27:6-7

➤➤➤| THEIR STORY |◄◄◄

The first rays of sunlight slanted across the sand, holding just the slightest hint of the heat they would bring by noon. The tabernacle—the special tent where God's very own presence sometimes stayed—was still just a large shadow in the early morning light.

Mahlah, Noah, Hoglah, Milkah, and Tirzah held hands as they waited near the tabernacle entrance. The sisters had gotten up early to make sure they would be first in line when Moses and the other leaders came out to hear the people's requests, problems, and complaints. They had something important to ask him.

After the Israelites escaped Egypt and began their journey through the desert, God established laws for his people. One law said that when a man died, everything he owned would be divided between his sons. Mahlah, Noah, Hoglah, Milkah, and Tirzah's father, Zelophehad, had recently died. But he didn't have any sons. And now it was up to his daughters to protect their father's name and memory—and their future.

A crowd was gathering as people came to hear the decisions Moses would make that day. A long line had formed behind the five sisters as the sun rose higher, and the air was now warm. At last, the crowd got quiet as Moses and the other leaders took their places near the tabernacle's entrance. Moses looked toward the people waiting to make their requests. He beckoned the sisters forward.

The people watching murmured in surprise at the sight of five young women coming to speak with Moses. He looked at the sisters, eyebrows raised. "What can I do for you?" he asked.

Mahlah took a deep breath. Her sisters pressed in close to her. "Our father, Zelophehad, recently died," she told Moses. "He had no sons—just us five daughters. But why should his family name disappear when we are here to carry it on? Let us be our father's heirs and divide his property among us. When we reach the promised land, whatever land would have been our father's should belong to us."

More surprised murmurs rose from the crowd. *Daughters inheriting their father's property?* Some people in the crowd smiled mockingly at Mahlah's last words. *These silly girls still believe in the promised land!*

Moses looked at the sisters for a moment, his expression serious. Then he nodded. "I will take your case to the Lord," he said. "We will see what he has to say about this matter."

The sisters thanked Moses and went home to wait. They knew that when Moses finished listening to everyone who needed to speak to him that day, he would go to the tabernacle and meet with God. The sisters sang as they prepared their evening meal, happy to know their request would be considered by God himself.

The next day, Moses called the sisters back to stand before the people again. "The Lord says that the daughters of Zelophehad are right," he told everyone. "They should inherit their father's property, and when we reach the promised land, Zelophehad's land will be divided among them. From now on, if a man dies without sons, his daughters will inherit everything he owned."

Mahlah, Noah, Hoglah, Milkah, and Tirzah smiled and thanked God for his answer. They had asked for his help, and he had changed the law.

THEIR STORY

We don't know much about Mahlah, Noah, Hoglah, Milkah, and Tirzah—they only appear (briefly) twice more in the Bible, once to clarify how their inheritance would be affected when they got married, and once to mention that when the Israelites finally reached the promised land, they did get the land that would have belonged to their dad. But we can guess that when this story took place, they were probably very young women or girls, since none were married yet. Women and girls then usually couldn't get jobs or make their own money to live on; they depended on their fathers, husbands, or other male relatives. Since the sisters' father had died, they had no brothers, and they weren't married, they may have worried about how they were going to live and who was going to protect them and provide for their future. God showed them compassion and favor by telling Moses to change the law. With property of their own, the sisters would have resources to live on and invest for their future.

THEIR GOD

Have you ever worried about what was going to happen to you, or felt impossible obstacles are in your way? When we're in the middle of a difficult situation, it can be hard to see how things could change. The five sisters faced a society and laws that didn't make room for them and put them in a bad position. They may have started out feeling like there was nothing they could do. But God gave them courage to go to Moses and ask for the law to change. He helped them have faith they would one day receive everything God had promised to their people and their family. And he spoke to Moses and brought about the change the sisters needed. God is a good Father who takes care of his children, in Bible times and today.

> READ ABOUT ZELOPHEHAD'S DAUGHTERS IN NUMBERS 27:1–11; 36:1–12; JOSHUA 17:4.

RAHAB

STRENGTH TO CHANGE SIDES

[Rahab said,] "I know that the Lord has given you this land. . . . The Lord your God is God in heaven above and on the earth below."

JOSHUA 2:9, 11

->>>| HER STORY |<<<-

Rahab stood by one of the windows of her house, eyeing her guests. The two men were eating food she had just served them, trying not to draw attention, but they weren't fooling her. Their accents gave them away. They had to be Hebrews, the group camped across the Jordan River from Rahab's city, Jericho. Rahab's house was built into the city wall, with windows that faced outside the town, and people often paid to stay with her. For weeks, Rahab's guests had been talking about the Hebrews—how their entire nation walked across the dry bottom of the Red Sea, walls of water on either side of them. How they completely destroyed the armies of two powerful kings. How they worshiped a mighty God who made these things possible. Rahab had heard the fearful whispers of her neighbors in the streets and the marketplace. Everyone in Jericho was terrified of what the Hebrews might do to their city. And now two of them were here, in her house.

No doubt the men had been sent as spies to look at Jericho's defenses and take a report back to their leader. If Rahab turned them in to the king of Jericho, she might get a reward. And it was her duty as a citizen of Jericho; these men were her enemies. Though as she watched them, she thought about everything she had heard about their God. The Hebrews'

God had power not just in their land but in the lands of their enemies. He even had power over the earth itself. Rahab was used to looking out for herself. But just for a moment, she allowed herself to wonder what it would be like to have Someone so powerful watching over her, providing for her.

A noise outside the house caught Rahab's attention. She looked out the door to see a group of men turning onto her street. The king's men! Someone must have seen the two Hebrews entering Rahab's house and come to the same conclusion she had. Now these men were here to capture the spies.

Rahab quickly moved away from the window, making her decision. "Hurry!" she hissed at the two spies. They looked up at her, startled. "The king of Jericho has sent men to capture you!" She ran to a door at the other side of the room and yanked it open, revealing steps that led to the roof. "Quick! I'll hide you."

The men did as Rahab told them. She followed them up to the roof, where she had been drying flax she planned to make into cloth. She made the men lie down and quickly spread the stalks of flax over them, hiding them from view. Then she hurried back downstairs, just in time to hear pounding on her door.

Rahab straightened her clothes, checking to make sure no pieces of flax stuck to her clothing. She took a deep breath and went to answer the door.

"Where are the two men who came to stay here?" one of the king's men demanded. "They are spies! Bring them out now!"

"Spies?" Rahab said, hoping her voice wasn't shaking. "Yes, two men did come here earlier. But I didn't know where they were from! And they just left—they wanted to leave the city before the gates close at dusk. I don't know where they went, but if you hurry, you might catch them!"

The king's men hurried toward the city gates. Rahab closed her door and stood with her back against it, letting out a huge sigh of relief. She waited a few minutes, then went to the window, looking up and down the street to make sure there weren't any king's men—or nosy neighbors—lingering nearby. Then she went up to the roof.

"I got rid of the men who came to capture you," she told them. "But you better stay here tonight."

The men sat up, flax poking out from their clothes and hair. "Thank you for protecting us," one of them said.

"I've heard enough about your God to know he is the ruler of the heavens and the earth," Rahab told them. "Everyone here is afraid of your people because your God is going to give you this land, and no one can stand in his way. But please show kindness to me and my family, like I've shown kindness to you today. Please spare us when you take over the city."

The men looked at each other, then nodded. "We will repay you for what you have done today," they said. "If you don't tell anyone about us, we'll be kind to you when we come back."

Early the next morning, Rahab dropped a rope through one of her outer windows so the spies could climb down the wall and escape the city. Before they left, the men handed her a red cord. "Tie this in your window when we come to take the city," they told her. "That way our people will know to leave you alone. You and any of your relatives who are in this house with you will be safe."

The men climbed down the rope and disappeared into the early morning shadows. Rahab held tightly to the scarlet cord. There was no going back now. Soon she would be starting a new life, with a new people—and a new God.

→»»| HER WORLD |«««-

According to tradition, Rahab was an innkeeper in Jericho. Since her house was built right into the city wall, it would have been in a good spot to get business from travelers. Most of Rahab's guests were likely traveling merchants, people who went from town to town selling items. These people would pass on news and stories as they moved from place to place. So Rahab likely would have been one of the first people in Jericho to hear about the Hebrews and the things God had done for them.

The Bible tells us Rahab was a prostitute, someone who made money doing things with her guests that God said women should only do with their husbands. Archaeologists believe many women who ran inns in that time and place were also prostitutes. It's likely the Israelites would have looked down on Rahab because of her job—and most of all because she was a Canaanite. As we've seen before, the Israelites had a habit of looking down on outsiders. But the Bible tells us Rahab started a new life with the Israelites and seems to have been accepted by them. She eventually married an Israelite man named Salmon. Some people believe he was one of the spies Rahab protected, but since the Bible doesn't name the two spies, we can't know for sure.

→»»| HER GOD |««←

We generally don't admire people who decide to switch sides, turning their back on their family and friends to join people who are going against them. But more than turning away from her people, Rahab was turning toward God. Many people in Jericho had heard the same things as Rahab, but only Rahab made the choice to serve God.

Sometimes being on God's side might make us unpopular or mean we must give something up. Rahab lost her home and likely many of her friends. But God was faithful to her and gave her a new beginning. He didn't hold her mistakes against her or look down on her because of her past. He even gave her a place in Jesus's family tree! Rahab was the great-great-grandmother of David, one of Israel's most famous kings and an ancestor of Jesus.

Jesus is waiting to give you your own new beginning. When you join his family, your past failures—whatever you might be ashamed of or embarrassed about—are covered by his love and grace. You can be completely free to move forward in a new life with him. And the best part is, he gives you a new beginning each and every day. His love goes on forever!

READ ABOUT RAHAB IN JOSHUA 2; 6:17–25; MATTHEW 1:5.

DEBORAH

A STRONG LEADER

Deborah, a prophet, the wife of Lappidoth, was leading Israel at that time. She held court under the Palm of Deborah ... and the Israelites went up to her to have their disputes decided.

JUDGES 4:4-5

->>>| HER STORY |<<<-

Deborah leaned back against the trunk of the date palm tree and sighed. She shaded her eyes with a hand and looked into the distance. There was a small cloud of dust on the horizon, slowly getting nearer. Deborah nodded with satisfaction. She had been coming to sit under this tree for so long that her fellow Israelites called it the Palm of Deborah. She enjoyed its shade as she listened to the arguments and requests the people brought to her. With the wisdom God gave her, she decided what should be done in each case. Sometimes God spoke to her so clearly that she could pass his exact words on to the people. God had called her to be his prophet as well as Israel's leader and judge. It was a difficult job, but Deborah knew her people desperately needed to hear God's words. They had forgotten him and begun worshiping other gods, so God had allowed them to be conquered by their enemies. Jabin, a Canaanite king, ruled over Israel now. His army commander, Sisera, terrorized the people with his iron chariots. But that was about to change.

A bee buzzed around Deborah's head before zipping toward a blooming shrub nearby. Deborah smiled. Her name meant "bee," and the little creatures always reminded her that the place she lived was a land flowing with milk and honey—the land God had promised to give his people when he freed them from slavery in Egypt. God stayed faithful to his people even

when they were unfaithful to him. He had saved them from their enemies many times before, and he was about to do it again.

The dust cloud Deborah had been watching was now close enough for her to see two people in it—her messenger and the man she had sent him to fetch. They hurried to her. "Here is Barak son of Abinoam, my lady," the messenger said.

Barak greeted Deborah respectfully. "You sent for me, my lady?"

Deborah gazed at the man standing before her. He had a reputation as a great warrior and a respected leader. He had traveled a very long way to see her. His journey would be worth it, though, because she was about to speak God's very own words to him.

"This is what God says to you, Barak," she said. Barak's eyes widened, and he leaned forward expectantly. "'Go, gather ten thousand men from the tribes of Naphtali and Zebulun and take them to Mount Tabor. I will bring Sisera and his chariots to fight a battle with you by the Kishon River, and I will give you victory over him.'"

Deborah's messenger smiled with excitement. This was the rescue the Israelites had been praying for! Barak stood tall, his shoulders back, but there was a hint of doubt in his eyes. "I'll go, but only if you come with me, Deborah."

Deborah frowned. Barak had been given a direct command from God, and here he was, putting a condition on his obedience! "I will go with you," she said, crossing her arms. "But you will not get any honor from this victory. God will make it so that Sisera is defeated by a woman."

Barak looked uncomfortable, but he didn't protest this time. Deborah got up and walked away from the palm tree, motioning for Barak to follow. There was much to be done.

→»»| HER WORLD |««←-

Deborah lived during a time of difficulty for the Israelites. God had given them Canaan, just as he promised, but the people had not kept their promises to God. They ignored the way God wanted them to live and were influenced by some of the most evil and harmful customs of the nations around them. Israel got caught in a vicious cycle (some call it the Cycle of Judges): they forgot God; God allowed them to be conquered by their enemies; they cried out to God for help; God sent a leader, or judge, to save them; they forgot God; and the cycle started all over again.

Deborah was the fourth judge to save Israel, and the only woman. It was very unusual in that time and place for a woman to be the ruler of a country—Deborah was one of the very few women to lead Israel in its entire history. But it's clear the people respected and trusted her as their leader and also as a prophet. Again, God was showing that he chooses whoever he wants to work through, no matter their status in the eyes of people.

Some judges were military leaders, who helped the Israelites win battles against their enemies and drive them out of their land. Others, like Deborah, primarily helped the people live in peace and order together. But Barak still wanted Deborah to come with him to battle. Perhaps he wanted to prove to his army and the rest of the people that he was acting on God's orders, or maybe he wanted Deborah near so she could speak to God for him. Or maybe he just felt braver with Israel's leader nearby.

HER GOD

Because she was a woman, no one expected Deborah would grow up to lead her entire nation. So she most likely didn't receive any of the special training or education many rulers would have gotten. But somehow she became known as a person who could help people resolve difficult arguments or figure out a solution to a tough problem. How did this happen?

God gave Deborah wisdom—a knowledge that goes deeper than being clever or learning things from books. In the Bible, wisdom means knowing how things work: first, understanding that God is central and most important; then, knowing how everything else in life falls into place around him. Wisdom means understanding the right way to live and how to please God.

READ ABOUT DEBORAH IN JUDGES 4–5.

JAEL

STRENGTH IN BATTLE

Most blessed of women be Jael, the wife of Heber the Kenite,
most blessed of tent-dwelling women.

JUDGES 5:24

->»»| HER STORY |«««-

The calm inside Jael's tent was shattered by the sound of pounding footsteps outside. She rushed to the tent entrance, her heart beating fast. Had her husband been injured at his forge? No; she could still hear Heber's blacksmith's hammer ringing, just out of sight on the other side of the great oak tree.

A man was coming toward her tent, running like there was an army chasing him. Jael and her family had heard about the great army of Israelites that Barak son of Abinoam had been gathering. Heber had shaken his head at the news. He did his best to stay friends with both the Israelites and King Jabin, as he didn't want to get caught up in the battle.

But now the battle had come straight to Jael. She gasped as she recognized the running man. It was Sisera, the commander of King Jabin's army! Jael had seen him a few times, when he'd come with jobs for Heber. He had a reputation for being a cruel and ruthless man, and Jael had never liked the way he'd looked at her or the other women in her community. While he didn't have his iron chariot, and he was covered in dirt and blood, she was sure it was the same man. But Sisera wasn't going to Heber now, as any visitor should. He was coming to Jael's tent.

She clenched her fists. A man coming to a woman's tent was up to no good. She whispered a prayer for protection and courage. Then she stepped forward to meet Sisera.

"Come in, my lord," Jael said to the army commander. "Don't be afraid." She was trembling with fear herself, but she felt it was best to take charge of the situation. Sisera may have lost a battle, but he was still as dangerous as before—maybe even more so. He would be angry and embarrassed by his defeat and would probably be looking to take those feelings out on the nearest target, which right now was her.

Sisera rushed into the tent without hesitating or mentioning Heber at all, confirming Jael's suspicion that his intentions were not good. He sat down, panting. Jael covered him with a blanket. "Give me some water," Sisera gasped.

Jael quickly opened a container of milk. Sisera would see it as a better drink than water, and she hoped it would help keep him calm until she decided what to do.

"Keep watch at the entrance of the tent," Sisera ordered her. "If anyone comes by and asks if someone is in here with you, say no."

Jael nodded and stood in the tent entrance, anger rising along with her fear. Sisera was asking her to risk herself for him, something no guest should ask of a host. Behind her, Sisera's breathing got slower and deeper. She peeked over her shoulder. He was fast asleep.

Should she run for help? But what could any of her family do? And if Sisera woke up while she was gone, he might go into one of her relatives' tents and threaten them. Even if she and her family escaped Sisera, who knew what he would do to someone else? She had heard the stories about him. No. This man was too dangerous to let live. Barak should never have allowed him to escape the battlefield. Now Jael would have to finish the job for him.

She slipped back into the tent and found a tent peg and hammer. Then she quietly approached the sleeping man.

When it was over, Jael stood outside her tent, trembling from head to foot. Another man was coming up to the tent, sword in hand. But Jael recognized this man as well—it was Barak.

"Come," she said, holding the tent flap open. "I will show you the man you're looking for." Barak looked puzzled but poked his head into the tent. His eyes widened at the sight of Sisera lying on the ground, a tent peg

save the Israelites from the people who were oppressing them and controlling their land? She couldn't wait to share the news with her husband and ran to find him.

"Manoah!" the woman called, running into their home. "You'll never believe what just happened! A man of God came to me—he looked awesome and terrifying, like an angel!" Manoah's eyes widened as his wife told him what the angel had said. He wanted to hear the angel's instructions for himself, so he prayed, asking God to send the man to them again.

Soon after, the woman was once more in the field when she had the same feeling that someone was with her. The angel was back! "Let me run and get my husband!" she said. She raced to find Manoah. "He's here! The man of God is back!" she yelled. Manoah hurried after her to where the man stood waiting.

"How should we raise our son, who you've told us will be born?" Manoah asked the stranger.

"Your wife must do as I told her," the man replied. He repeated the instructions he had given the woman.

"Please stay so that we can prepare a meal for you," Manoah said, wanting to treat this special guest with honor. His wife stared at him. Didn't he realize this must be an angel? He wouldn't eat a meal like an ordinary person.

"I will stay, but I won't eat anything," the man replied. "But you may bring the food as a sacrifice to God."

"What is your name?" Manoah asked. "So that we can honor you when your prophecy comes true."

The stranger smiled. "Why do you ask my name? It is too wonderful for you to understand."

Manoah brought his offering and placed it on the altar, then lit the fire to burn it. The flames leaped higher and higher, and suddenly the stranger stepped into the fire! He rose up in a swirl of flames and disappeared.

Manoah and his wife fell with their faces to the ground. "We have seen God!" Manoah cried. "We're doomed!"

The woman felt awe and amazement, but she also felt the deep peace she'd experienced the first time the stranger had appeared to her. "Don't worry," she told her husband. "If God wanted us to die, he wouldn't have accepted our offering or told us all these things about the future."

The woman got to her feet. The field looked the same as it always did—except for the altar, now black and scorched. The woman watched the smoke rise toward heaven, just as her prayers had risen to God. He had answered, and her life would never be the same.

HER WORLD

The Bible doesn't tell us the name of the woman in this story. According to ancient Jewish tradition, her name may have been Zlelponi or Zlelponith. Some believe she was the woman named Hazzelelponi who is mentioned in 1 Chronicles 4:3. Some people believe these names are related to the Hebrew word for angel, *zel*, since the woman was given a special message by an angel.

Like Deborah and Jael, this woman lived during a time when the Israelites' land and lives were being controlled by an enemy nation. During this time, it was the Philistines, people related to the Greeks who had invaded Canaan from the sea. The Philistines had five major cities—Ashdod, Gaza, Ashkelon, Gath, and Ekron—each with its own ruler. The Philistines became Israel's biggest enemy from this time on. They were such a force in the region that it is still named for them today; the modern name "Palestine" comes from "Philistia," the land of the Philistines.

The woman's miraculous son, who she named Samson, was one of Israel's judges. He was kind of like a biblical superhero—he had superhuman strength, which he used to defeat and humiliate the Philistines. You can read Samson's story in Judges 13–16.

HER GOD

In ancient Israel, a woman was not considered as reliable a witness as a man. Perhaps this was why Manoah asked God to send his messenger again rather than taking his wife's word for what she had seen. But God sent his angel to Manoah's wife rather than to him—twice! Even when Manoah finally met the angel, he only repeated what he had already told the woman. Clearly, God felt she was worthy of receiving this special visit and message. And we see in this story that the woman responded to God in faith. She didn't question the prediction she would have a son after many years of being unable to have children. She didn't even freak out when the angel revealed his supernatural nature, because she trusted God's words about her future.

Most of us probably won't be visited by an angel in our lifetimes, but God still speaks to us in many ways. The most common way is through his Word, the Bible. Though it was written many, many years ago, it still matters for our lives today. God invites you to get to know him through his Word—and through Jesus, who is called God's living Word (see John 1:1).

READ ABOUT SAMSON'S MOTHER IN JUDGES 13.

NAOMI

STRONG COMFORT

"I went away full, but the Lord has brought me back empty. . . . The Lord has afflicted me; the Almighty has brought misfortune upon me."

RUTH 1:21

⟶≫| HER STORY |≪⟵

The whole town of Bethlehem was buzzing with the news. "Naomi is back from Moab! But Elimelek, Mahlon, and Kilion have not returned."

Naomi walked her hometown's familiar streets with her head down, trying not to think about how different things were from the day she'd left. Not so much the town of Bethlehem itself—though there were plenty of familiar faces missing, as well as some new buildings and others that had been recently repaired after the long famine. No, the biggest change was in Naomi herself. When she'd left, her husband, Elimelek, had been at her side, along with their sons Mahlon and Kilion. They had been nervous and worn out from the hard times they'd been through, but they'd been hopeful the move to Moab would mean better things for their family. Elimelek had told jokes as they went, making the boys laugh and Naomi smile. For the first time in a long time, she'd felt life might live up to the promise of the name her parents had given her, which meant "pleasant." But now—

"Don't call me Naomi," she snapped at the next group of women she saw whispering about her in a doorway. "Call me Mara—bitter—because God has made my life very bitter. I went away full, but the Lord has brought me back empty. Why call me Naomi? There is nothing pleasant about my life now. God has made terrible things happen to me."

RUTH

A STRONG REDEEMER

*The women of the town said to Naomi, "Praise the Lord,
who has now provided a redeemer for your family! May
this child be famous in Israel. May he restore your youth
and care for you in your old age. For he is the son of your
daughter-in-law who loves you and has been better to you
than seven sons!"*

RUTH 4:14–15, NLT

➤➤➤| HER STORY |◄◄◄

Ruth washed herself with a damp cloth, wishing she could wipe away the fluttering nervousness from her stomach and chest. A faint melody drifted through the air. It took Ruth a few moments to realize it was Naomi humming as she swept the doorstep of their tiny house. Ruth smiled. It had been a long time since she'd heard Naomi hum.

"Almost done?" Naomi bustled into the room, leaving her broom by the door.

"Yes, just finished." Ruth wrung out the cloth and hung it over the edge of the basin, then began to dress in the clothes Naomi had laid out for her—the best she had, clothes she hadn't worn since her husband, Mahlon, died. She could hear Naomi behind her, rummaging around by her sleeping mat.

"Here." Naomi came up to Ruth, a tiny jar in her hands. She pulled out the stopper, and a beautiful fragrance filled the air. Naomi sniffed. "I don't even know why I brought this from Moab," she said. "There wasn't enough left to sell. I was going to throw it away, but at the last moment I decided to keep it, as a reminder of Elimelek and happier times." Her eyes grew misty, but her face didn't twist with bitterness like it used to. Ruth laid her hand on Naomi's. The older woman sniffed and wiped her eyes. "Well," she said briskly, "I'm glad I kept it after all. I pray it will help bring you new happiness."

"Thank you." Ruth hugged Naomi, then daubed on some perfume. She covered her hair and straightened her clothes. "How do I look?"

Naomi smiled. "Perfectly beautiful," she said. She took Ruth's hands. "Don't worry. Just do exactly as I told you."

Ruth nodded. "I will." She took a deep breath, then hurried from the house, giving Naomi one last wave. The sun was sinking as she walked quickly along the route that had become so familiar over the last months, toward Boaz's fields, where she had found not only more than enough food for herself and Naomi to live on, but a kindness and acceptance she hadn't expected.

Naomi insisted God himself had led Ruth to Boaz's field on the first day she had set out to pick up grain behind the workers who were harvesting barley. She believed Naomi must be right. Boaz had been so kind to Ruth from the moment they'd met. She had gone to Boaz's field to glean the barley that was left after the workers were done harvesting. He had told her to follow right behind the young women who were tying the grain into bundles, instead of making her wait until the bundles had been carried away, as was the usual custom. She'd even seen his workers pull out handfuls of barley and drop them on purpose, which she was sure Boaz had told them to do. Boaz had shared his water and even his meal with her, incredible hospitality to show to a stranger and a foreigner! He'd told Ruth he admired her for her loyalty to Naomi.

Naomi had been overjoyed when she saw how much grain Ruth brought home and heard about everything Boaz had done. It turned out that Boaz was one of Elimelek's closest relatives and might be able to buy back Elimelek's property for Naomi. Naomi thought Boaz would also be willing to marry Ruth and provide a secure home and future for both women.

So now Ruth was here, at the threshing floor, the place where Boaz and his workers were winnowing—removing—the chaff from the barley they'd harvested. She found a place to hide and watched while the men finished their work and enjoyed a celebratory meal. She knew Boaz would sleep at the threshing floor to guard the grain from thieves.

Ruth wrapped her shawl tightly around her and shifted from side to side to ease her cramped muscles. Time crawled by. Finally, the men quieted, and she saw Boaz walk off by himself and stretch out near the pile of grain, wrapping himself in his cloak.

Ruth waited a few minutes more, until she was sure Boaz was asleep, then she crept over to him and uncovered his feet. As she lay down near them, her heart pounded.

She'd been sure she'd lie awake all night, but she must have dozed off, because the next thing she knew she was being woken by a sudden movement and Boaz's gasp of surprise. "Who are you?" he whispered hoarsely.

"I am your servant Ruth," she said back softly, her mouth so dry she could barely speak. "Please spread the corner of your cloak over me, since you are a guardian-redeemer of our family."

Boaz was silent for what felt like hours. Finally, he gave a soft, surprised chuckle. "The Lord bless you, my dear," he said. "You are showing even more family loyalty by not going after a younger man. Now don't worry about a thing. I will do whatever is necessary, for everyone in town knows you are a woman of noble character."

Ruth's cheeks warmed at Boaz's praise. He explained that they would first have to give a closer relative the chance to buy Elimelek's land and marry Ruth, but she wasn't worried about that. She knew God had brought her to Boaz's field on that very first day, and he had brought her here tonight. She lay back down near the kindest man she had ever met and waited for the new day to come.

→»» | HER WORLD |«««←

When God brought the people of Israel into the land he had promised to give them, he gave them a lot of laws about how they should run

HANNAH

STRONG IN PRAYER

In her deep anguish Hannah prayed to the Lord, weeping bitterly. And she made a vow, saying, "Lord Almighty, if you will only look on your servant's misery and remember me, and not forget your servant but give her a son, then I will give him to the Lord for all the days of his life."

1 SAMUEL 1:10–11

HER STORY

The area around the tabernacle, the special tent where God's people worshiped him, was filled with the scent of celebration feasts and the sound of laughter and songs of praise. But for Hannah, one sound always drowned out the merriment and took away her appetite.

"Thank you, husband," Penninah cooed as Elkanah handed her a platter heaped with meat from his yearly sacrifice to God. "Ooh, it's so heavy—you are so generous to me and all our children!" She glanced slyly at Hannah out of the corner of her eye. "I can't carry this by myself; I'll need two of our strong sons to help me!"

After making a fuss as her two oldest sons carried the platter to where her other children sat, Penninah was finally gone and Hannah could approach Elkanah, who was also her husband. Elkanah smiled apologetically at Hannah as he placed an extra-large helping of the best cuts of meat onto her plate. Just as she did every year, Hannah thought back to the early days of her marriage, when it had been just her and Elkanah, young and in love and believing they had a happy future ahead of them. If only Penninah had never come into their lives. If only many things had been different.

stay out of Nabal's way. They were all used to this—Nabal was a quick-tempered man who often acted without thinking. But this time his wicked foolishness might cost the lives of their entire household. He had given a serious insult to a famous warrior who was traveling with his own army. In addition, many people in Israel believed David was the true king, ever since Samuel had anointed him. But the old king, Saul, refused to give up the throne and was trying to kill David. And now Nabal had put himself on the side of David's enemy.

Abigail thought quickly and came up with a plan. It was risky, but it might calm David's anger and keep him from taking revenge on Nabal's household. "Come quickly," she called to her servants. She instructed them to help her pack a large gift of food for David and his men. "And work quietly; don't let Nabal know what we are doing," she warned them.

Once the food was packed, Abigail sent it with some servants to David's camp. "I'll be right behind you," she promised them. She got ready to travel, then took a deep breath and mounted her donkey, riding in the direction her servants had gone.

Sooner than she would have liked, Abigail rode into a ravine and saw a large group of men coming down the other side. She'd heard David had about six hundred men in his army, and it seemed that most of them were coming toward her, swords at their sides and grim expressions on their faces.

Abigail got off her donkey and walked up to the man who rode at the head of the group. From his air of command and the way the other men were looking at him, she knew he must be David. She bowed low before him to show respect and began to speak quickly. "Pardon me, my lord," she said. "Please listen to what I have to say. I accept all blame in this matter. Pay no attention to Nabal; his name means 'fool,' and that's what he is. I never saw the men you sent. Let all your enemies be as cursed as Nabal is!"

Abigail gestured at the food she had sent ahead of her. "Here is a gift I have brought you. The Lord is with you and will surely do what he has promised for you. When you become the leader of Israel, you won't want people to say that you took vengeance for yourself and did unnecessary violence. And please remember me, your servant, when God brings you success!" She remained still, bowing low before David, holding her breath.

For a few long moments, the only sound was the snorting of Abigail's donkey behind her. She glanced up at David's face. All at once his stern expression relaxed, and she felt a ripple of relief pass through the men crowding behind him.

"Praise God for sending you to meet me!" David exclaimed. "Your good sense has saved me from committing murder. Before you came, I was planning to kill every man in Nabal's household. Thank you for your gift. You may go home in peace."

Abigail let out her breath in a quiet sigh of relief. She thanked David, bowed to him again, and quickly made her way home, having made a peace treaty with a future king.

⟶⟫⟫⟫| HER WORLD |⟪⟪⟪⟵

This story takes place shortly after the death of Hannah's son Samuel. Samuel led Israel as a judge for many years, but then the people decided they wanted to have a king like the other nations around them. So God chose a man named Saul to be Israel's first king. Saul started out following God, but when he decided to ignore God and go his own way, God chose a new king for the nation, a shepherd named David. Saul did not want to give up the kingship and recognize David as the new king. Instead, he tried to kill David. During this story, David and the men who'd joined his army were on the run from Saul.

When Abigail got home and told her husband what had happened, the shock made him very ill (perhaps he had a stroke), and he died ten days later. When David heard that Nabal had died, he sent a message to Abigail asking her to marry him. David had already married two other women, and he went on to marry at least five more women after her. Abigail and David had one son together, who was known by two names: Daniel or Kileab.

HER GOD

In this story, David had every right to be offended—he had worked hard to help someone, and instead of being grateful, that person had insulted him terribly. But David was about to let his anger lead him into doing something terrible when Abigail stepped in.

When we feel hurt or offended by someone, it can feel good to lash out at that person with everything we have. We want to make sure they get what they deserve for what they did to us. But God is not like that. Over and over, the Bible describes him as "slow to anger." Abigail reflected God by coming to David to make peace. She hadn't done anything wrong herself, but she took on the responsibility of correcting the offense. Her peacemaking saved the lives of her husband and servants, and her calm response helped David realize that his own anger was out of proportion and saved him from doing something he'd deeply regret. No wonder Jesus calls people who work for peace "children of God" (Matthew 5:9)!

READ ABOUT ABIGAIL IN 1 SAMUEL 25.

THE WIDOW AT
ZAREPHATH

STRENGTH TO TAKE A RISK

*The word of the Lord came to [Elijah]: "Go at once to
Zarephath in the region of Sidon and stay there. I have
directed a widow there to supply you with food."*

1 KINGS 17:8–9

⇥ HER STORY ⇤

The ground was dry and dusty by Zarephath's town gate. The dust coated the hands and clothes of the woman who was gathering sticks just outside town. She straightened up and stretched her back, shading her eyes against the sun. It had been beating down day after day for months, baking the earth, burning the crops, and drying up the rivers. The woman couldn't remember the last time she'd seen a cloud in Phoenicia, much less felt a drop of rain.

She squinted against the sun's glare. A shape had appeared on the horizon, coming toward her. She kept an eye on it as she continued to gather sticks for her fire. Soon, she could tell it was an Israelite man.

As a widow who lived alone with her young son, she normally would be wary of a strange man—especially a foreigner—but for some reason she felt sure this man meant her no harm. He looked tired and hungry; but then, who didn't, after so many months of famine?

"Would you please bring me a little water?" the man asked, leaning wearily against the town wall. The woman nodded and started toward her home to get it. "And a piece of bread, please."

The woman turned to stare at the stranger. Surely, he had seen that

95

THE SHUNAMMITE
WOMAN

STRONG IN WELCOME

[The Shunammite woman] said to her husband, "I know that this man who often comes our way is a holy man of God. Let's make a small room on the roof. . . . Then he can stay there whenever he comes to us."

2 KINGS 4:9-10

HER STORY

Bed, table, chair, lamp. The woman looked around the room she and her husband had built and furnished for a special guest. Elisha, one of God's prophets, often came by their house in Shunem on his travels. The woman knew that too often, her people didn't pay attention to what God's prophets had to say and even made fun of them or mistreated them. She had built this room to show Elisha that he and his message had a special place with her family.

The next time Elisha arrived to share a meal with the woman and her husband, she showed him and his servant, Gehazi, the room. "Lie down and have a rest," she invited them. "You are welcome for as long as you want to stay." Elisha looked pleased, and the woman went about her work, humming quietly.

A while later, Gehazi appeared. "Elisha would like to speak to you," he said. "Will you please come upstairs?" She followed him to Elisha's room.

The prophet smiled at her. "I want to thank you for your hospitality and the effort you've put into making us feel welcome," he said. "Is there anything we can do for you? I could speak to the king or the commander of the army for you, if you have a problem."

NAAMAN'S SERVANT

STRENGTH TO LOVE ENEMIES

Bands of raiders from Aram had gone out and had taken captive a young girl from Israel, and she served Naaman's wife. She said to her mistress, "If only my master would see the prophet who is in Samaria! He would cure him of his leprosy."

2 KINGS 5:2-3

➤➤➤| HER STORY |◄◄◄

The girl sorted through her mistress's beautiful clothing, checking each item carefully and placing it into piles for washing, mending, or folding and putting away. She worked as silently as she could, careful not to disturb her mistress, who was resting on a couch on the other side of the room. It was during quiet moments like this that she missed her family the most. She wondered what her parents and siblings were doing and if they thought about her and missed her—if they'd survived that horrible day when the Aramean raiders attacked their home. Sometimes she imagined the future she would have had if soldiers hadn't captured her, bringing her to Aram, where she became a servant to the wife of their greatest general, Naaman. She wouldn't have had clothes as lovely as the ones she was handling now, nor a house as big and fine as the one she helped clean, but perhaps she would have had a little home of her own—a husband, some children, her sisters nearby, her mother giving advice. The Arameans had stolen all of that from her too, when they'd stolen her away from everything she'd known and loved.

the palace where her nephews, Ahaziah's sons, lived. Her heart broke as she passed room after room where the young princes played or ate or slept, not realizing the danger they were in. Jehosheba desperately prayed that the whispers she'd heard weren't true, that her stepmother wasn't planning to kill her own grandsons and take the throne for herself. But knowing Athaliah, Jehosheba was very afraid. And from the moment she'd heard of that evil plan, Jehosheba knew there was little she could do to stop it. The queen mother would never listen to the daughter of one of her husband's other wives, especially one who'd married a priest of the religion she despised. However, Jehosheba also realized there was one thing she could do to save the royal line of David. A very small thing.

She burst into the royal nursery, startling the woman inside. But the baby she was holding didn't wake up. Jehosheba breathed a sigh of relief. The other rumor she'd heard had turned out to be true. Ahaziah's wife Zibiah had just given birth to a son.

"You need to come with me, now!" Jehosheba whispered to the baby's nurse. The woman started to protest, but Jehosheba cut her off. "There's no time to explain. The child's life is in danger. You have to help me save him!"

She grabbed the nurse's arm and pulled her out of the room and along the halls. The nurse stopped resisting and followed close behind her, pulling her shawl over the baby to hide him. Jehosheba prayed he would stay quiet until they escaped.

Catching the sound of booted feet coming down the hall, Jehosheba pulled the nurse into an alcove. The two women huddled against the wall, holding their breath, as a group of palace guards passed with swords drawn. Tears spilled down Jehosheba's face. So it was true. Those men were on their way to kill the king's sons so Athaliah could take the throne. For a moment she wondered if she should have tried to save more of her nephews. Was there something she hadn't thought of?

But she had no time for such thoughts, not if she was going to save the child she had with her. Athaliah would hunt down the other princes no matter where they might hide, but there was a chance she didn't know

HULDAH

STRONG IN HIS WORD

Hilkiah the priest, Ahikam, Akbor, Shaphan and Asaiah
went to speak to the prophet Huldah.

2 KINGS 22:14

→»» | HER STORY |«««-

Huldah stood by her window, the sunlight red against her closed eyelids as she listened to God. She still couldn't believe God had given her such a wonderful gift. She had always loved to listen to stories of the great prophets like Miriam, Deborah, Elijah, and Elisha—who God spoke to directly, who carried messages from God to his people—but she hadn't dared to dream she might become one herself. Yet God had chosen her. He spoke his very own words to her, and it was her responsibility to tell people what God wanted them to know. It was not a privilege she took lightly.

She opened her eyes and thanked God for the message he had just given her—intended for the king. She didn't know how she would deliver it, but God would show her in his own time, like always.

As she began to go downstairs, Huldah heard a knock on the door. She went back to the window and peered down into the street. Her eyes widened when she saw the men standing at her door. The high priest, the court secretary, and King Josiah's personal adviser—important people in the kingdom! It had been a long time since the kings of Judah had cared enough about God's words to come visit a prophet. Though many of the things King Josiah had done made her hopeful that he was different from his father and grandfather. He had even begun to repair God's temple,

nodded at her sisters, and the girls sprang into action. They had been secretly borrowing tools from neighbors for days as they went about their errands, and now hurried to gather them from various hiding places around the house. One of the sisters brought out the food and water she had packed early in the morning, before anyone else got up. "Ready?" the oldest sister asked. The others nodded. "Let's go."

The girls marched out of the house and joined their father at the wall. He gave them a puzzled smile. "Is that for me?" he asked, looking at their basket of food. "I already grabbed my meal. Plus, I can't take a break yet, my dears. I've barely begun."

"No, Father," said the oldest daughter. "It's for us." She and her sisters took out their tools. "We've come to help. Will you show us what to do?"

Shallum stared at his daughters. "But—"

"Women don't do building work," one of the daughters finished for him. "Father, we know. But God has given you daughters instead of sons, and the wall must be repaired. We're sure we can quickly learn, if you will show us. Will you let us help you?"

Shallum looked at his daughters, then at his section of wall, then at his neighbors' sections. He chuckled and shook his head. "The Lord works in mysterious ways," he muttered. "Well, come on, then."

The daughters worked alongside their father every day. At first, their neighbors stared and whispered, but as Shallum's section grew taller and taller, until it caught up to everyone else's and even passed some, disapproval gave way to acceptance and even respect.

The wall's progress did not go unnoticed by Judah's enemies, and the builders carried news of threats along with bricks and water. Soon, Nehemiah ordered the people to work in shifts, some building while others stood guard. Everyone was to carry a weapon with them. Shallum tried to persuade his daughters to stay home. "We can't stop now!" they said. "We are not afraid."

Shallum sighed. "I suppose at least this way I can keep an eye on you," he muttered. "Who knows what you'd get up to if I left you at home. But stay close."

"Yes, Father," the girls agreed. They strapped on their borrowed weapons and followed their father out to continue the work.

⟶⟩⟩⟩| THEIR WORLD |⟨⟨⟨⟵

When the Nebuchadnezzar, ruler of the Babylonian empire, conquered the land of Judah after Josiah's son became king, he destroyed much of the capital city, Jerusalem, and took most of the people captive and back to Babylon. But after many years, the kings who came after Nebuchadnezzar allowed some of the people of Judah to return to their homeland. Things were very difficult for them there—with the wall around the city in ruins, they were open to enemy attack. Nehemiah was a Jewish man who was also a trusted adviser of the king of Persia (the Persians had conquered the Babylonians some time before). He asked the king for permission to come to Jerusalem and help the people rebuild. Nehemiah served as the governor of Judah for a time and then returned to his work with the Persian king.

In that time and culture, building and construction was considered work for men only. The Bible doesn't tell us how or why Shallum's daughters ended up building alongside their father, but it's likely Shallum didn't have any sons. It was urgent that the people repair Jerusalem's walls as quickly as possible, so they needed everyone to pitch in and lend a hand. The Bible probably mentions Shallum's daughters because it was so unusual for women to do this kind of work.

⟶⟩⟩⟩| THEIR GOD |⟨⟨⟨⟵

When the people of Israel made their covenant with God way before he led them into the promised land, God told them what would happen if they didn't keep up their part of the agreement. But sadly, the people did not pay attention to this warning. Over the years, God sent many prophets to keep giving the people warnings and to try to persuade them to fix their relationship with God and go back to following him. But the people ignored God again and again. Finally, God allowed them to experience the terrible consequence of being conquered and taken away from their land.

But even after all that, God didn't stop loving or caring about his people. He was with them when they were captives far from home (as we'll see in the next story), and he eventually brought them back to their own land to start over.

Sometimes people feel they have made so many bad choices and made such a mess of their lives that there is no more hope, no going back—that God has given up on them. But that is never true. God tells us through his Word that his love does not give up and does not stop. Jesus came to earth to live and die as a human as the ultimate sign of God's unstoppable love. No matter what we do, no matter how far we run away from God, Jesus will always come find us (see Matthew 18:12–14).

READ ABOUT SHALLUM'S DAUGHTERS IN NEHEMIAH 3:12.

ESTHER

A STRONG QUEEN

Esther sent this reply to Mordecai: . . . "I will go to the king, even though it is against the law. And if I perish, I perish."

ESTHER 4:15–16

➤➤➤| HER STORY |⫷⫷⫷

Esther stood still as her ladies-in-waiting helped her put on her most beautiful royal robes, trying to meet their worried glances with a reassuring smile. It was hard when she felt light-headed, not only with nervousness at what she was about to do, but from fasting for the last three days.

Esther held out a hand so one of her maids could put bracelets around her wrist. Though she couldn't stop her hand from trembling; the maid clasped it and held it tight until she was able to hold it still. Grateful tears stung Esther's eyes. Her maids had been loyal to her and guarded her deepest and most dangerous secret since before she had become queen. They had fasted with her, and now they were doing their best to prepare her for what lay ahead.

Finally, she was ready, bejeweled and glittering from head to toe like the queen she was. Esther still couldn't believe that she, the adopted daughter of a palace official, had been chosen by the king out of all the beautiful young women who had been gathered from throughout his kingdom. Her cousin and guardian, Mordecai, had told her that she had been made queen for a special purpose—for what she was going to do today.

If that was true, she would do her best. She would do her best to walk into the king's presence without fainting from fear and lack of food. She would do her best to ignore the fact she was breaking the law by going to see the king without an invitation. She would do her best not to think about Queen Vashti and what happened the last time one of the king's wives made him angry. She would do her best to save the lives of her people.

Mordecai had offended the king's favorite adviser, Haman. Haman had grown to hate Mordecai so much that he wanted to kill him—and wipe out his entire ethnic group, the Jewish people. Haman had convinced the king that the Jews were a threat to his reign, and the king had made a law allowing his subjects to kill Jews on a certain date. At Mordecai's insistence, Esther had hidden her Jewish identity since coming to the palace, but she had no idea how much longer she'd be able to keep that secret.

Esther took a deep breath, and then another. She hugged each of her ladies-in-waiting. Then she set off on what felt like an endless journey from her chambers to the king's hall.

As she walked, she thought about her father and mother, lost so many years ago that her memories of them were fuzzy and faint. She thought about how long it had been since someone had called her by her Jewish name, Hadassah. She thought about Mordecai and her life with him before the king's officials came to take her to the palace. She remembered the year of beauty treatments with the other young women who were hoping to be queen, and the moment she found out that King Xerxes had chosen her. And even though she tried not to, she thought about how it had been thirty days since the king had last sent for her—long before he had passed the terrible law that would doom her entire people to distinction. Had he somehow found out she was a Jew? Did he want her to die as well?

Though the walk had seemed endless when she'd started, all too soon she found herself facing the entrance to the king's hall. This was it.

Esther took another deep breath, straightened her shoulders, and held her head high. If this was to be her last act on earth, she would die with dignity, doing what was right. She entered the room.

The queen fixed her eyes on the base of the throne at the far end of the hall, staring at the king's feet—she didn't dare look at his face. She could hear a few gasps and whispers at her unexpected appearance, but she kept focused and walked straight ahead.

She stopped a respectful distance from the throne and bowed low before the king, holding her breath.

She waited. The throne room was silent.

Esther looked up.

The king was holding out his golden scepter as a sign of his favor, that he was pleased to see her. He was smiling.

Esther's breath rushed out in a sigh of relief. She wanted to collapse into a puddle on the throne room floor, but she made herself stand and go to the king, touching the tip of the scepter. The first part of her mission was a success. It was not her day to die after all.

→»»| HER WORLD |«««←

While some Jews chose to go back to Judah to rebuild, Esther was part of a group that stayed in Persia instead. Both of her parents died when she was young, and she was raised by her cousin Mordecai. Mordecai seems to have had a fairly important position in King Xerxes's palace, so it's possible his family didn't want to give up the wealth and status they'd achieved.

King Xerxes's first queen was named Vashti (although some Bible scholars believe that Vashti, which means "best," "desired," or "beloved," might have been her title, and that her actual name was Amestris. Other scholars think that Vashti was her Persian name and Amestris was her Greek name. Xerxes is also known by the name Ahasuerus). Some years before Esther's story takes place, Xerxes threw a huge party and decided that he wanted to show off Vashti, who was very beautiful, to his guests. He sent a messenger to Vashti ordering her to put on her royal crown and come to him, but she refused. We don't know exactly why Vashti didn't want to obey the king, but it's possible she felt it wasn't appropriate for her to go to the party, or she was worried the king would do something to embarrass her. Either way, her refusal made Xerxes so furious that he banished her.

Eventually, Xerxes decided he wanted a new queen. His advisers encouraged him to gather a large number of young women from all over his kingdom and choose a queen from among them. Esther was part of this group, and Xerxes chose her. Mordecai encouraged Esther to hide her Jewish identity from the king and most of the palace, though it's likely that some of Esther's closest attendants knew, because they helped carry messages between Esther and Mordecai.

After Esther's courageous visit to the king, she revealed her Jewish identity and exposed Haman's evil intentions. The king punished Haman, and the Jewish people were saved.

->>>| HER GOD |<<<-

One of the most interesting things about the book of Esther is that it doesn't mention God by name a single time. But if you look closely, you can see God at work throughout the entire story. God put Esther in an important position and gave her the strength and courage she needed to use her position to save the lives of her people—even though it meant risking her own. God was with his people who stayed in Persia even as he was with the people who went back to Judah.

Sometimes we may feel like God is far away or even that he's disappeared from our lives. Often, we don't understand what he is doing or why he allows certain things to happen. But God has promised that he will never leave us or abandon us (see Hebrews 13:5). Esther's story teaches us that God is always at work, always caring for the people he loves, even if it seems to be from behind the scenes.

READ ABOUT ESTHER IN THE BOOK OF ESTHER.

WISDOM

A STRONG FOUNDATION

Choose my instruction instead of silver, knowledge rather than choice gold, for wisdom is more precious than rubies, and nothing you desire can compare with her.

PROVERBS 8:10-11

➵➵➵| HER STORY |⟨⟨⟨⟨⟨

Wisdom left her beautiful house with its seven graceful pillars and hurried out into the streets, heading toward the city gates. She had spent hours preparing her feast, and now all the delicious dishes were laid out on a beautifully set table. All that was missing were the guests. Wisdom ran up to the top of a hill overlooking the city, calling out her invitation to everyone she met: "Come to my banquet! Leave your foolish ways behind; learn to use good judgment."

She paused at every crossroads, boldly speaking truth to travelers passing by. She knew that so many of them needed her: people who were inexperienced and naive, who didn't know how much they didn't know; people who thought they were already smart and clever, who liked to make fun of everything; and people who were so busy chasing the things they thought they wanted that they didn't have time or energy to care about doing the right thing. "Listen to me!" she shouted. "I only speak what is true and right. I can show you how to really live."

She reached the city gates, where people were buying, selling, and doing business. "The gifts and rewards I give are better than gold and jewels," she told them. "I can tell you how to find true wealth and honor."

Wisdom climbed up to the city walls, spread her arms wide, and raised

her voice again. "I have always walked close beside God," she said. "I was there when he made everything. If you know, love, and respect God, you will have me beside you every day of your life, to help you know what is right and do what is right. That is the way to truly live—that is real happiness, real treasure. Come and see!"

Some people listened and followed Wisdom back to her home, joining her splendid feast. Some people turned away, or pretended not to hear, or laughed mockingly at her. Wisdom ate and drank and brought out beautiful gifts for her guests, but she never forgot the people who remained outside. Tomorrow, she would prepare another banquet and go out into the streets again, tirelessly inviting people to leave the path that ends in death and follow her into life.

HER WORLD

The woman in this story is not a historical figure. But she's not fictional either. She is a personification—God's wisdom described as a woman. Wisdom appears as a woman in the writings of King Solomon, the son of King David. Solomon was known for being a very wise person and a good writer—he wrote all or part of three books of the Bible (Proverbs, Ecclesiastes, and Song of Songs). Solomon used lots of imagery and figurative language to describe the truths he wanted to impart. Wisdom is one of his most well-known images. Early in Solomon's reign, God appeared to him in a dream and offered him anything he wanted. Solomon asked for wisdom and discernment, or the ability to make good choices, so that he could rule God's people well (see 1 Kings 3:5–15). Though he didn't always use his wisdom perfectly, Solomon remained interested in the subject throughout his life. Wisdom was one of the most important gifts God gave Solomon.

HER GOD

Many people think of wisdom as a synonym of intelligence or knowledge, but the kind of wisdom King Solomon wrote about in Proverbs doesn't

to their skills and abilities. She saw the image of God in each one of them, and she wanted to bring out the best in them and help them grow.

She greeted her children with hugs and kisses as they ran into the kitchen. Each of them was a precious gift from God, and it was her and her husband's responsibility to help them learn and grow in love, wisdom, and good relationships with God, other people, and the world.

The woman's husband came into the kitchen next, swinging the children into the air. The couple sat down to share their meal, talking over their plans, hopes, and challenges for the day. They were partners and trusted each other completely. Their love was strong, always looking to do what was best for the other person. When it was time for her husband to go out, he kissed his wife and whispered words he told her almost every day: "Many women do amazing things, but you outshine them all!"

The woman was busy the rest of the day at home and in the world, considering various business opportunities and making investments. She bought and sold, made and mended, talked and listened.

As busy as she was, she did not forget those in need. She saw the image of God in them as well. She remembered how generous God was with her, and that made it easy to be generous and share with others.

The woman understood that time was a gift from God and used it as wisely as she could. Even though she had many things to do, she knew it was important to take time to rest and also to be quiet before God, speaking to him and listening for his voice. She prayed throughout the day, asking God for help to make the right choices and show kindness to everyone she encountered, always thanking him for all he gave and did.

It was dark again by the time the woman had finished her daily tasks. She felt tired but fulfilled, happy to know she had spent her time well.

→»»| HER WORLD |««←

The story of the woman of valor—also known as the wife of noble character or the virtuous woman—appears in a poem that appears at the end of the book of Proverbs. It's an acrostic poem—its twenty-two stanzas each begin with a letter of the Hebrew alphabet. Some Bible scholars believe it was written by Solomon, and others believe it was written by a king named Lemuel (and some people believe that Lemuel is a pen name for Solomon!).

Some scholars think this woman is closely related to the woman Wisdom, or even the same personification appearing in a different form. (Note both Wisdom and the woman of valor are described as more valuable than rubies [see Proverbs 8:11; 31:10].) The woman of valor shows what it looks like to live wisely in several different areas of life.

The acrostic form of poetry was often used to describe and praise heroes who did mighty and amazing things. This woman is portrayed as a hero of wisdom, who puts into practice the lessons of Proverbs.

→»»| HER GOD |«««-

The Hebrew words that are translated "wife of noble character," "virtuous and capable wife," or "virtuous woman" (among other ways!) in English are *eshet khayil*, "woman of valor." (Boaz also used them to describe Ruth in Ruth 3:11.) The English word *valor* means courage and bravery; the Hebrew word means that too, but also means doing the right thing, caring for those who depend on you, and having honor and strength.

This poem is often held up as a pattern and example for girls and women to follow. This woman of valor demonstrates many wonderful characteristics that are good for anyone to have. But it's important to remember that God doesn't want us to be superwomen who are good at everything and run around being perfect all the time. The woman of valor shows us what it looks like to walk in God's wisdom in a certain time, culture, and lifestyle. But the central truth is that wisdom comes from God. If we ask him, he can show us what it looks like to be women of valor today.

> READ ABOUT THE WOMAN OF VALOR IN PROVERBS 31:10–31.

THE BELOVED

LOVE AS STRONG AS DEATH

Place me like a seal over your heart, like a seal on your arm; for love is as strong as death, its jealousy unyielding as the grave. It burns like blazing fire, like a mighty flame. Many waters cannot quench love; rivers cannot sweep it away. If one were to give all the wealth of one's house for love, it would be utterly scorned.

SONG OF SONGS 8:6-7

→»»| HER STORY |«««-

The woman pushed open the shutters and leaned out the window. The winter rains had finally stopped, and the air smelled clean and fresh and full of new life. Everywhere the woman looked, plants were pushing up through the earth, unfurling new leaves and reaching toward the sun.

Something new was growing in the woman's heart also, budding and blossoming like the lilies and crocuses she could see in her garden. She scanned the horizon, bouncing on her toes with anticipation.

There! He was coming! A strong, athletic figure was running up to the house, bounding like a gazelle. The woman's heart pounded in her chest. Suddenly shy, she stepped back from the window, closing the shutters to hide her burning cheeks.

Soon a gentle tapping sounded on the shutters, and a deep voice spoke, sending a thrill from the top of the woman's head to her toes. "My darling, my beautiful one, come with me. The winter is past; the rains are over. The earth is full of flowers and song. My darling; my beautiful one, come with me."

Joy filled the woman's heart and made her forget her shyness. Her beloved belonged to her, and she to him. She would follow him anywhere.

The woman got up and ran out of her house and into her beloved's arms.

→»»| HER WORLD |«««-

This woman is the main character in the biblical book called Song of Songs, or Song of Solomon. This book has challenged and puzzled Bible scholars for a very long time! Most believe that at least most of it was written by King Solomon, but there are many different ideas about its characters, its story, and its meaning. Some think that the characters were real, historical people, and others think they are symbolic—representations or personifications like Wisdom in the book of Proverbs. For a long time, scholars thought the book was an allegory—a symbolic story about God's love for his people. Most people today see it as a story about human romance and marriage (though, since God made us in his image, all human love is a reflection of God's love). Other people believe that the book is a story about two people, the woman and King Solomon. And there are people who believe that the story is about three people, and King Solomon is actually the villain! And still others believe that the book isn't one story at all but a collection of poems about love and marriage.

Another interesting thing about Song of Songs is that the female characters speak much more than the male character(s). This was very unusual for the time and culture in which it was written. The beloved woman was not afraid or ashamed to talk about what she wanted and how much she loved her husband. She was an active participant in her romance and a full partner in her marriage.

→»»| HER GOD |«««-

The Bible makes it clear that God created romantic love and marriage. They are good and beautiful gifts from him. When a husband and wife respect and love one another, they are showing a special and unique picture of Jesus's love for his people (see Ephesians 5:21–33).

In our broken world, it's easy to develop a broken view of romantic love. Lots of the things we read, watch, and hear seem to tell us that romantic love is the most important thing in life, that you should spend all your time and energy looking for it, and that if you don't have it, you're missing out big time. Many, many people spend a huge amount of time, energy, and money trying to make themselves attractive or looking for a special relationship or feeling bad about themselves because their soulmate hasn't shown up yet. But the woman of Song of Songs calls on her fellow young women to promise her "not to awaken love until the time is right" (Song of Songs 3:5, NLT). Those who have not received God's gift of romantic love should trust that he wants what is best for them, and he will bring a spouse into their lives if and when it's right. It's also important to remember that romantic love is only one of the many good gifts God gives us, and it's much better to enjoy the things God has already given you than to focus on the things he hasn't.

God also shows us in this book of the Bible that he celebrates human romantic love. When spouses are trying to serve God and one another in their relationship, they can and should celebrate their love without any shame—just with joy, delight, and thankfulness for God's good gift.

READ ABOUT THE BELOVED IN THE SONG OF SONGS.

ELIZABETH

STRONG JOY

When Elizabeth heard Mary's greeting, the baby leaped in her womb, and Elizabeth was filled with the Holy Spirit. In a loud voice she exclaimed: "Blessed are you among women, and blessed is the child you will bear! . . . Blessed is she who has believed that the Lord would fulfill his promises to her!"

LUKE 1:41–42, 45

→»»| HER STORY |«««-

Elizabeth paused in wiping the table to stretch her aching back. She rubbed her rounded belly and smiled. It wasn't easy being pregnant at her age, but she didn't mind. Every ache was a happy reminder of how God had taken away her many years of sadness and shame.

The baby inside her shifted, calm and quiet as she completed her daily tasks. A son, the angel had told Elizabeth's husband, Zechariah. She still couldn't believe it. Gabriel, an angel who stood in the very presence of God, had come to Zechariah while he was doing his work as a priest in God's temple and told him that he and Elizabeth would finally have a son—an amazing miracle.

Zechariah had told Elizabeth all of this through signs and writing because the angel had made him unable to speak after he'd initially doubted God's message. Elizabeth had shaken her head and affectionately laughed when Zechariah wrote out why he was mute. "You'd think a man who has spent his life serving in God's house wouldn't be so surprised when God shows up there and speaks to him!" she'd said, kissing Zechariah's wrinkled cheek. He'd given her an embarrassed smile and patted her hand.

Elizabeth teased Zechariah that his silence was finally giving her some peace after so many years of listening to him talk, but the truth was she missed the sound of her husband's voice. Gabriel had said he would be able to speak once the baby was born—another reason to be excited. Her friends and the midwife said it wouldn't be long now. All those friends were grandmothers or even great-grandmothers now, long past having babies of their own. They chuckled and shook their heads at Elizabeth's incredible pregnancy, but she knew they were happy for her.

"Elizabeth, shalom aleichem—peace to you!" a young, clear voice called from the doorway. The baby in Elizabeth's belly suddenly leaped, making her grab the table for support. She smiled as she saw who was standing at the door—her young relative Mary, who lived in Nazareth, a four-day journey away. Along with surprise and joy at the unexpected visit, a strong feeling of peace and love and certainty came over Elizabeth. She knew it must be the spirit of God, and he had just told her something amazing—Mary would soon give birth to God's promised Savior!

"Mary!" she exclaimed, hurrying to hug and kiss the girl. "You are blessed by God, and the little baby in your womb is blessed too! What have I done to deserve such an honor, that the mother of my Lord would come all this way to visit me? As soon as I heard your greeting, the baby in my womb leaped for joy—he already knows who you carry! You are blessed because you believed in God and in the wonderful things he is doing."

Mary's eyes filled with tears. She softly laid a hand on Elizabeth's belly, awe and wonder filling her face. Elizabeth held the younger woman, gently patting her back and marveling at what God was doing in and through them, two humble women.

→»»| HER WORLD |«««-

After the Old Testament ends, God didn't send any prophets, and there's no record of him appearing to his people—this is a time sometimes called "the four hundred years of silence." But God broke his silence in dramatic fashion by sending an angel called Gabriel to Israel with a pair of very special messages. The first was to Elizabeth's husband, Zechariah. Elizabeth was not only married to a priest but was from a family of priests herself. The priests had many special responsibilities and privileges. It was their job to care for God's temple and lead the people in following and worshiping God. Gabriel appeared to Zechariah while he was performing a special task—burning a fragrant mixture called incense in the holiest part of the temple. A priest might get chosen for this job only once in his life, so it was an extremely important moment. He would have prepared himself to be close to God, but he probably never expected God would send an angel to speak to him! And he certainly wasn't prepared for the angel's message. Elizabeth and Zechariah are another couple in the Bible who were unable to have children for many, many years.

When Elizabeth's son was born, her friends and relatives expected her to name him after his father or another relative. They probably would also have expected him to become a priest like Zechariah. But, following God's instructions, Elizabeth and Zechariah named their baby John, which means "the Lord has shown favor." John became a prophet, and one with a very specific task: announcing the coming of the Messiah. The Messiah (which means "anointed one") was a Rescuer who had been talked about by prophets centuries before, and many Jews were waiting for him to appear. John's job was to tell God's people that the Lord was showing them favor, and their wait was over—Jesus was on his way.

⟶≫⟩| HER GOD |⟨≪⟵

When Zechariah heard God was going to give him and Elizabeth a miraculous child, he reacted with doubt. That's understandable—from a human standpoint, it was a difficult thing to believe! But Elizabeth seems to have responded with gratitude and joy. She showed the same joy when Mary visited her. Elizabeth seems to have known about Mary's pregnancy without being told; the Bible says that when she heard Mary's greeting, she was filled with the Holy Spirit (see Luke 1:41). This probably means God spoke to her like he did to his prophets, supernaturally telling her Jesus was going to be born. God's long silence was over. He was speaking to his people again through angels and prophets, and he was giving them the best news of all—Jesus was coming to save them.

And one day he will return again to heal all the brokenness in the whole world and make everything beautiful and new. We can share Elizabeth's joy—our Rescuer is on the way.

READ ABOUT ELIZABETH IN LUKE 1:5–80.

MARY,
THE MOTHER OF JESUS

STRONG FAVOR

Mary said: "My soul glorifies the Lord and my spirit rejoices in God my Savior, for he has been mindful of the humble state of his servant. From now on all generations will call me blessed, for the Mighty One has done great things for me—holy is his name."

LUKE 1:46-49

HER STORY

Mary laid her head on her relative Elizabeth's shoulder, crying tears of joy and fear and anxiety and relief and amazement—everything she'd been feeling since an angel appeared in front of her a few weeks before and given her news that would change her life forever. He'd told her she would become pregnant, before she and her fiancé, Joseph, started their life together as husband and wife. God would make this possible, because her baby would be the Son of God. Sometimes, it didn't seem real. But Elizabeth had greeted her as the mother of her Lord before Mary had spoken a word about her pregnancy. Joy filled Mary's heart as well, washing away all her fears and worries about what the future might bring.

Mary wiped her eyes, and Elizabeth drew her into the house. The two women sat together, and the joy in Mary's heart bubbled over. She found herself singing a song of praise she had made up on the long journey from her home in Nazareth to Elizabeth's home near Jerusalem. Elizabeth listened, her eyes shining.

Based on the time and culture Mary lived in, we can be fairly sure she was young, probably no older than fifteen or sixteen. (Most girls at the time were married by their mid-teens.) Mary had promised to marry a carpenter named Joseph. Their relationship was a bit different than many modern engagements, because Mary and Joseph's engagement was an agreement between their two families, and it was legally binding. They were already husband and wife in the eyes of the law, even though they hadn't yet started living together as a couple. (Some Bible translations say Mary was "pledged" or "betrothed" to Joseph instead of "engaged" to him to reflect this difference.)

The Bible doesn't tell us what Mary looked like. Numerous artists have depicted her with blue eyes and golden hair, but it's far more likely she had dark hair and eyes and brown- or olive-toned skin, like many people who live in the Middle East today. Many people imagine she was very beautiful, but the Bible doesn't say one way or the other. Since the Bible does say God is more interested in people's hearts than their appearance (see 1 Samuel 16:7), most likely physical beauty was not one of the things God was looking for when choosing the mother of Jesus.

->»| HER GOD |«<-

When the angel Gabriel appeared to Mary, he called her "favored" by God. Does that mean Mary was like a teacher's pet, better behaved or more spiritual than others? If we look at the entire Bible, we see God's favor has a lot more to do with God than it does with the people he favors. That is, God pours out his favor and blessing on people because he is gracious and loving, not because they are perfect or especially deserving.

However, the Bible tells us Mary was ready to receive God's favor and blessing with faith and joy. She didn't respond with doubt, the way Zechariah did when Gabriel appeared to him, even though what the angel told her was even more incredible and miraculous. She didn't point out to Gabriel all the ways an unexpected pregnancy would make her life difficult. (It would have been considered very shameful for a girl to get pregnant before marriage. When Joseph found out Mary was pregnant and he wasn't the father, he wanted to divorce her, until an angel told him Mary was carrying God's Son. It's possible that people who didn't believe Jesus was really God's Son would have gossiped about Mary or even treated her badly.) Instead, Mary said, "I am the Lord's servant. May everything you have said about me come true." She recognized God was doing something beautiful and exciting and miraculous through her, and she responded with joy.

God poured out his favor on Mary and gave her the strength to be Jesus's mother. And because of Jesus, you can receive that same strength and blessing from God. He loves you and has work for you to do. He is ready to pour out his favor on you.

READ ABOUT MARY, THE MOTHER OF JESUS IN
MATTHEW 1–2; 12:46; LUKE 1–2; JOHN 2:1–11; 19:25; ACTS 1:14.

ANNA

STRONG PROMISES

There was also a prophet, Anna.... She never left the temple but worshiped night and day, fasting and praying. Coming up to [Mary, Joseph, and baby Jesus] at that very moment, she gave thanks to God and spoke about the child to all who were looking forward to the redemption of Jerusalem.

LUKE 2:36-38

→»»| HER STORY |«««–

Anna smiled as she entered the temple courtyard. Now that she was an old woman, she knew what was truly important in life. The activities that used to keep her busy when she was younger were no longer as interesting; now, what made her truly happy was spending her time speaking to God and praising him. And there was no place she would rather be than in God's house. Anna knew God was everywhere—she felt his presence and heard his voice speaking to her no matter where she went—but the temple was special. It was a visible reminder that God lived among his people, and he met with them here in a distinct way. Only a few months ago, Anna had been praying in the temple when the priest Zechariah burst out of the sanctuary, unable to speak, waving his hands wildly in the air. Anna later heard that Zechariah had seen an angel in the Most Holy Place. And then she'd heard Zechariah's wife, Elizabeth, had become pregnant and given birth to a son, even though both the priest and his wife were almost as old as Anna. An angelic messenger and a miraculous birth, after so many years of waiting—it sparked such excitement in Anna's heart!

Anna slowly made her way through the temple courtyard, praying silently. *You promised us a savior, Lord,* she prayed. *Many have forgotten or stopped believing, but I haven't. I know you are faithful, that you keep all your promises. Please show me how you are working today.*

A loud voice, ringing out all the way across the courtyard, interrupted Anna's prayers. She smiled. Her old friend Simeon couldn't speak softly if he tried. But today he sounded especially excited. She moved toward his voice, trying to glimpse him through the crowd of worshipers. Finally, she caught sight of him, standing near a young couple who were holding a baby. Anna's smile widened. She loved seeing the tiny babies who were brought to the temple to be dedicated to God. She moved closer, Simeon's words becoming clearer.

"Sovereign Lord, as you have promised, you may now dismiss your servant in peace," Simeon boomed. "For my eyes have seen your salvation!"

Anna gasped. Simeon had shared with her that God revealed he wouldn't die before seeing the Messiah, the Savior God had promised to send his people. Simeon was bending toward the young woman next to him, his hand resting gently on her baby's head, tears streaming down his face. Anna felt tears stinging her own eyes as she hurried toward the little group. *Could it be . . . ?*

As Anna approached, Simeon turned to her and beamed. Anna felt God's Spirit with her, filling her up, telling her that it was true, that God had kept his promise, that her people's long, long wait—her wait—was finally over. Tears of joy spilled from her eyes, and she lifted her hands high, praising God with her whole heart.

The young mother smiled and placed the baby in Anna's arms. "His name is Jesus," the young woman said. Anna looked down at the tiny bundle, awe filling her heart. He didn't look any different from the hundreds of other babies she'd seen here in the temple. But she knew beyond any doubt he was the one, God's anointed—the Messiah.

She held the baby a moment longer, then gave him back to his parents. Her heart was overflowing with the wonderful news, and she couldn't wait a moment longer to share it with anyone who would listen. God's Savior had come!

HER WORLD

The Bible says Anna was a prophet, someone who received messages from God and shared them with others. After centuries without a prophecy, the story of Jesus's birth is filled with people who were empowered by God's Spirit to speak God's words. Zechariah, Elizabeth, Simeon, and Anna were all witnesses to the very new and special thing God was doing—sending his own Son to live among his people and be their Savior.

Besides her gift of prophecy, the Bible only gives us a few other details about Anna. Her name is the Greek version of the Hebrew name Hannah. She was a widow who was married only seven years before her husband died. She was an old woman, but Bible translators disagree on her exact age; some think Luke 2:37 tells us she was eighty-four years old, while others believe it says she lived eighty-four years after her husband's death, which would make her over a hundred years old. The Bible says "she never left the temple" (see Luke 2:37), which probably means she went there often, like how we might say, "She's always going to the temple."

HER GOD

Things had not been easy for the Israelites (also called the Jewish people) during the years between the Old and New Testaments, and by Anna's time, they had been conquered yet again, this time by the Roman Empire. They felt very sad and angry about being under Roman control, and it was probably hard at times to remember and believe in God's promises—that he still loved them, that they were still his people, that one day he would deliver them and make things right. But Anna was one of the people who had not given up hope. She went to the temple day after day to speak and listen to God. God gave her the strength to continue to hope and not to give in to sadness or loneliness. He gave her the incredible privilege of meeting Jesus very early in his life and enabled her to immediately recognize him as God's Savior. She then shared that good news with everyone she could.

Do you ever feel like things are dark and hopeless, either in your own life or in the world around you? Remember that God always keeps his promises (see Psalm 146:6). When things start to look bleak, ask someone you trust to help you find some of God's promises—and ask God for the strength to believe and hold on to them.

READ ABOUT ANNA IN LUKE 2:36–38.

THE SAMARITAN
WOMAN AT THE WELL

A STRONG WITNESS

Leaving her water jar, the woman went back to the town and said to the people, "Come, see a man who told me everything I ever did. Could this be the Messiah?" . . . Many of the Samaritans from that town believed in him because of the woman's testimony.

JOHN 4:28-29, 39

HER STORY

The woman slipped between the buildings of Sychar as she made her way to the town well, trying to use the buildings' short shadows to protect herself from the midday sun. Many of her fellow townspeople were inside, resting during the hottest part of the day, but the woman was thirsty. So she settled her water jar and coil of rope more comfortably on her shoulder, pulled her head covering close around her face, and braved the hot stretch between the last building and the trees surrounding the well.

Suddenly, the woman pulled up short. There was a man sitting by the well. That itself wasn't surprising—it was a popular place for people to gather, rest, or pray—but this man wasn't from Sychar, or anywhere else in Samaria. The woman could tell he was Jewish.

What was a Jewish man doing here, resting by a well in a Samaritan town, looking comfortable and at ease? Did he not realize where he was? Jews and Samaritans had been at odds for centuries. Some Jews would even go out of their way to avoid Samaria when they traveled.

Well, the woman needed water, and that man didn't look like he was

going anywhere soon. She would just ignore him. She was sure he would do the same—as he'd consider a Samaritan woman not worth noticing.

The woman approached the well, careful not to look at the Jewish man, and set her water jar down. She began to tie the rope to the jar so she could lower it into the well.

"Will you give me a drink?"

The woman froze, her knot half tied. Had the man really spoken to her, or was she imagining things? She peeked up at him. He was looking at her, the trace of a smile on his lips.

"Why are you asking me for a drink?" she muttered. "You are a Jew, and I am a Samaritan woman."

The man's smile grew. "If you knew about God's gift and who is asking you for a drink, you would have asked me, and I would have given you living water."

The woman's brow wrinkled in confusion. What was this man talking about? "Sir," she said, "you have no rope or bucket to draw water with, and this well is very deep. How would you get this living water you're talking about?"

"Everyone who drinks this water"—the man gestured at the well—"will eventually get thirsty again. But people who drink the water I give them will never be thirsty. My water will be a fresh, flowing spring inside them, bringing them eternal life."

A longing rose within her, one she'd felt all her life. It felt a bit like the physical thirst she was feeling, but it went deeper—a thirst in her heart and soul.

"Sir, please give me this water," she said to the man. "Then I won't have to keep coming back to the well."

The man looked into her eyes. "Go, call your husband and come back," he said gently.

The woman looked down. Of course. This stranger wouldn't share his secrets with a woman. And he couldn't know what feelings the word *husband* stirred in her heart—grief, loss, shame.

"I have no husband," she told him.

down on the Samaritans for their mixed ethnicity and their mixed religion. Most Jewish teachers in Jesus's day would rather have gone thirsty than ask a Samaritan woman for a drink, much less begin a whole conversation with her.

→»»| HER GOD |«««-

The woman went to the well that day looking for water to quench her physical thirst, but she ended up finding so much more. Whatever the specific choices or circumstances that led her to that point, it's certain her past was painful. Life had not brought her satisfaction or fulfillment. Her spirit was dry and thirsty.

What was the "living water" Jesus offered the woman? He used the same words another time, when he was speaking to a lot of people in the temple. He said those who were thirsty should come to him and drink, and living water would flow from them. The Bible tells us "by this he meant the Spirit, whom those who believed in him were later to receive" (John 7:39). When we trust in Jesus to fix our broken relationship with God, God's Spirit comes to live inside us—flowing like a river in a desert, filling in everything that's missing or empty in our hearts, bringing life where there used to be death. That living water will also flow onto people we meet, bringing the life Jesus offers into their lives—just as it flowed from the woman at the well to her entire town.

READ ABOUT THE SAMARITAN WOMAN IN JOHN 4:1–42.

A HEALED WOMAN

STRONG HEALING

When [Jesus] saw her he said, "Daughter, be encouraged!
Your faith has made you well." And the woman was healed
at that moment.

MATTHEW 9:22, NLT

→»»| HER STORY |«««-

Someone's elbow jabbed into the woman's side, and she gasped in pain. Her eyes filled up with tears and she struggled to see. She felt so dizzy and weak that she could hardly walk . . . but that didn't stop her from pushing her way through the crowd as fast as she could. She was used to pain and weakness; they had been her constant companions for twelve long years. Ever since the day her bleeding had started and never stopped, caused by something more serious than a cut or injury. She could feel her life trickling away with each passing hour. That was why she was here, ignoring the rules that said she should hide herself away so her impurity wouldn't contaminate others. And she definitely shouldn't be touching people. She was making everyone she bumped into or brushed against unclean. But Jesus was so close; she couldn't pass up this opportunity. He was the only one who could help her.

She knew Jesus of Nazareth was a busy and important man. Many people wanted his attention and needed his help. Right now, he was following a well-dressed man who strode forward as if the crowd of people wasn't there, his servants shoving a path clear for him. She recognized him—it was Jairus, another important man and a Jewish leader. The woman also recognized the desperation on Jairus's face. She'd heard his daughter was

very sick. Jesus was Jairus's only hope too. The woman didn't want to get in the way and keep a little girl from being healed. She wouldn't take very much of Jesus's time.

"If I can just touch his robe, I will be healed," the woman whispered to herself. She repeated it over and over as she struggled to get close to Jesus and struggled to ignore the mocking voice in her mind. *You shouldn't be here. You're unclean. You don't deserve to be healed. You're a nobody.* She pushed the thoughts away. She knew Jesus could help her. She just had to get close enough to touch his robe.

There! A tiny space opened in the crowd between her and Jesus. The woman used the last of her strength to lunge forward, her hand stretched as far as it could go. Her fingers skimmed one of the tassels on the edge of Jesus's robe.

A beautiful, cleansing coolness washed through her from head to toe, like plunging into a rushing stream. Her vision cleared and her balance steadied. She took a deep breath, feeling strength flow into her body. The pain was gone.

"Who touched me?"

The woman froze in fear. Jesus was searching the faces in the crowd. A few steps ahead, Jairus pulled up short, looking back impatiently. The woman ducked her head, trying to hide from Jesus's eyes.

"Teacher, this whole crowd is pressing up against you," said Peter, one of Jesus's disciples. "Who *isn't* touching you?"

"No," Jesus said, still scanning the crowd. "Someone touched me on purpose. I felt healing power go out from me."

The woman knew she couldn't hide from Jesus. She stepped forward and knelt at his feet, her whole body shaking. "Forgive me, Teacher," she said. Her voice was barely louder than a whisper, but everyone had grown so silent that her words carried to the whole crowd. "I have been unclean and suffering for twelve years," she explained. "I spent all the money I had on doctors and did everything they told me, no matter how painful or unpleasant. Nothing they did helped. But I knew you could heal me, even if I just touched the edge of your robe." She kept her eyes on the ground, waiting for Jesus's response. Would he scold her for letting her impurity infect him and the whole crowd? Would he walk away in disgust?

"Daughter, be encouraged!" Jesus said, his voice as warm and healing as the morning sun. The woman looked up into his face. The Teacher was smiling at her, his eyes full of love. "Your faith has made you well. Go in peace."

⟫| HER WORLD |⟪

We don't know exactly what kind of sickness this woman had, but the Bible says she had been bleeding for twelve years. According to Jewish ritual law, bleeding was a sign of death and made a person impure or unclean, meaning they couldn't participate in religious ceremonies and had to remain separate from other people. Anything and anyone this woman touched would also become ritually impure and would have to be specially cleaned. So the woman had suffered for a long time, not just from the physical pain of her illness, but from the loneliness and shame that came from being seen as a source of death and impurity and from having an isolated life.

Bible scholars believe the woman likely touched a tassel on Jesus's outer clothing. Jewish men would wear four tassels on their robes that represented their ceremonial purity and devotion to God. When this dying woman reached for the symbol of Jesus's cleanness and closeness to God, instead of her impurity contaminating him, Jesus's life and purity healed her and made her clean.

⟫| HER GOD |⟪

The Bible says people who have faith "believe that [God] is real and that he rewards those who truly want to find him" (Hebrews 11:6, ICB). The sick woman believed Jesus was able to heal her—that he was so powerful, she would be healed by only touching his clothes. Jesus rewarded her faith by healing her body.

Having faith in God doesn't mean believing he will always do what we want—it's believing he is real, he loves us, and he will always do what is best for us. Sometimes it's hard to believe those things. But the Bible tells us we can even ask God to help us have faith in him (see Mark 9:24).

Sin—everything we do, say, or think that goes against what's right and harms our connection with God—is like a sickness in our souls. Like bleeding that won't stop, sin brings pain and death to our hearts. When our hearts reach out to Jesus in faith, he heals our souls and gives us his life.

> READ ABOUT THE HEALED WOMAN IN MATTHEW 9:20-22;
> MARK 5:25-34; LUKE 8:43-48.

JAIRUS'S
DAUGHTER

STRONGER THAN DEATH

[Jesus] took her by the hand and said, "My child, get up!"
Her spirit returned, and at once she stood up.

LUKE 8:54–55

➵➵➵│ HER STORY │⫷⫷⫷

It was bad, she knew. Her parents kept telling her she would be better soon, that before long she would be taking walks with her father and learning to cook from her mother and laughing with her friends. But she could see the worry in their eyes, getting stronger by the day. And she could tell she was getting worse. She didn't feel much pain anymore. Instead she felt very weak, to the point she could barely move and could only stay awake for a few minutes at a time. It was also getting harder to swallow food, no matter how hard she tried just to please her mother.

When she'd first realized how sick she was getting, she'd been afraid, but she didn't feel afraid now. She was simply tired. So tired.

Her mother sat by her bed, holding her hand. She wanted to tell her mother not to cry, but she couldn't make her voice work.

"Hold on, my love," her mother whispered, her voice thick with tears. "Hold on, please. Your father has gone to find the Teacher, Jesus of Nazareth. He will be able to help you. Just hold on until they get here."

She tried to squeeze her mother's hand, but it was slipping away, or maybe she was the one slipping away. She wanted to hold on, but she was just too tired.

"Little girl."

That voice—it was somehow familiar, even though she was sure she'd never heard it before.

"Little girl, get up!"

And for the first time in a long time, she wanted to get up. Right now! She opened her eyes and discovered a man was holding her hand, a man with the kindest face she'd ever seen and eyes full of laughter. She sat up and bounced to her feet. "There you are!" he said, in that same voice. She laughed with joy. She felt so healthy and strong and full of energy! She wanted to ask the man a million questions and follow wherever he was going next.

The man looked over her shoulder. She turned to see her parents. Her mother was clinging to her father, one hand pressed to her mouth. The girl ran to their arms. They stroked her hair and her back. "You're here! You're alive!" they said over and over. "Jesus brought you back from death!"

She turned to look at the man who'd done more than just heal her—Jesus. He grinned at her. "I think this girl needs something to eat," he said.

She suddenly realized how hungry she was. "Yes, please!" she said, her stomach growling. Her parents laughed, their faces still wet with tears. She held out a hand to each of them and they walked out of her room together.

→»»| HER WORLD |«««←

The Bible tells us the girl in this story was twelve years old and her father, Jairus, was a leader of a synagogue, a Jewish congregation that worshiped together. When the girl got very sick, Jairus asked Jesus to come heal her. But before Jesus got to the girl's house, some people came to tell Jairus his daughter had already died. Jesus continued on, telling Jairus to have faith.

In that time, when someone died, friends, family, and neighbors would come to the person's house to grieve together. They would also hire professional mourners, who would help create a sad atmosphere by crying and wailing loudly and playing instruments. When Jesus got to Jairus's house, it was full of people and noise. Jesus told everyone to be quiet and only allowed the girl's parents and three of his disciples—Peter, James, and John—to be in the room when he raised the girl from the dead.

What did the girl in this story experience between the moment of her death and the moment when Jesus raised her to life? What did she remember about being dead after Jesus brought her back? The Bible doesn't tell us. In fact, though several people in the Bible had visions of heaven while they were still alive, the Bible does not let us know what the people who died and came back to life experienced while they were dead.

➤➤➤| HER GOD |◄◄◄

Are you afraid of death? You have good reason to be! Some people say death is a natural part of life, but the Bible tells us that isn't true. Death was not part of God's plan for us—it's the result and consequence of sin. It is right and normal for us to feel scared, sad, and angry when someone we love dies or when we face our own death. Jesus felt that way too! When one of his close friends died, he felt angry and cried with sadness (see John 11:33–35). When he knew he was close to dying himself, he asked God if there was any way to avoid it (see Matthew 26:39). Death is our enemy.

But the good news is that if Jesus is on our side, death can't defeat us. We don't know when we will die or what it will be like. But we can be sure Jesus will be right there with us, holding us tight. The Bible says that as soon as we die, we will arrive in the home Jesus has prepared for us in heaven (see 2 Corinthians 5:1–8). And one day Jesus will destroy death forever (1 Corinthians 15:26).

> READ ABOUT JAIRUS'S DAUGHTER IN MATTHEW 9:18–25;
> MARK 5:21–43; LUKE 8:41–56.

A CANAANITE WOMAN

A STRONG ANSWER

"Dear woman," Jesus said to her, "your faith is great. Your request is granted."

MATTHEW 15:28, NLT

→»»| HER STORY |«««-

The woman hurried along the street, desperately hoping she would find the man she was looking for. Sharp pains pierced her side, her breath came in gasps, and she could feel blisters forming on her feet, but she kept going, driven by the mental image of her daughter lying on the floor, limbs jerking in a seizure. Sometimes when she looked into her child's eyes, she saw something else inside—something terrifying. Her daughter needed help, and she would get it, whatever it took.

She reached the house she'd been told about and pounded on the door. Someone opened it, but she didn't pause to speak to them or even look at them as she rushed inside.

There! A group of Jewish men sat in the main room. The one in the center had to be the man she was looking for—the others hung on his every word. "Have mercy on me, Lord, Son of David!" she called out to him. "Please help my daughter—she is being tormented by an evil spirit and is suffering terribly."

The man only glanced at her briefly before returning to his teaching. Fine. She wasn't surprised—as a woman and a Gentile, a non-Jew, he would consider her unworthy of his attention. But she wouldn't give up easily. She

A WOMAN
CAUGHT IN SIN

STRENGTH FOR A SECOND CHANCE

Jesus . . . said to the woman, "Where are your accusers?
Didn't even one of them condemn you?"
"No, Lord," she said.
And Jesus said, "Neither do I. Go and sin no more."

JOHN 8:10–11, NLT

→»»| HER STORY |««←

She struggled against her captors, pulling against their grasp so hard she thought she might pull her shoulders out of their sockets, but their grip was like iron. They marched her through the temple courtyard toward where a crowd sat, listening to one of the rabbis.

"Let's see him talk his way out of this one," sneered one of the men gripping her arm.

"That's right," said another. "We'll trap him between the law of Moses and the law of the Romans."

The woman's face burned with shame. Not only was she about to suffer for what she had done, but these men—religious leaders and teachers—were going to use her sin to harm someone else too.

Jesus of Nazareth. She'd heard about him, and how the people were fascinated by Jesus while the leaders hated him. How he taught like no other rabbi and did amazing miracles. Well, it would take a miracle to help her now. One she didn't deserve.

The crowd fell silent, staring as the leaders marched her to the middle of the group and forced her to her knees, then stood back, leaving her alone and shivering in the early morning air.

"Teacher," one of the leaders said to Jesus, somehow making the respectful title sound like an insult, "this woman was caught betraying her husband. The law of Moses says women who do this should have stones thrown at them until they die."

Actually, the law of Moses says both men and women who do this should be stoned, the woman thought. But the leaders had grabbed only her.

"What do you say?" The leaders smirked at Jesus, springing their trap. If Jesus said they shouldn't stone the woman, it would look like he didn't respect the law of Moses. If he agreed she should be stoned, he would appear harsh, and he might also get in trouble with the Romans, who said they were the only ones who could give the death penalty.

The silence grew so heavy the woman could almost feel it pressing down on her shoulders. It seemed like everyone was holding their breath, waiting to see what Jesus would say.

But he didn't say anything. Instead, he bent down and began writing in the dust with his finger. The woman couldn't see the words.

"Well?" her accusers demanded. "Should we stone her or not?"

Jesus finally straightened. "All right," he said. The woman gasped in fear. "But let anyone of you who is without sin throw the first stone." Then he bent down and kept writing in the dust.

The woman heard a movement and tensed, waiting for the first stone to strike her. But it never came. She heard more movements, but still no stones. After several minutes, she looked up. The men who had brought her here were gone. She glanced over at Jesus, who was still writing.

Eventually, he sat up and looked at her. "Where did they go?" he asked. "Didn't even one person stay to condemn you?"

"No, Lord," she whispered. Guilt and shame washed over her, making it hard to keep looking at him.

But he was meeting her eyes with compassion. "Then I won't condemn you either," he said. "Go now, and don't sin anymore."

The woman stared at him in astonishment. Just like that, it was over?

She got up and stumbled away, the crowd parting for her. As she left the temple, gulping in deep breaths, her mind spun with wonder as she gazed at the rising sun. She had thought her life would end today. Instead, a new life was beginning.

➤➤➤| HER WORLD |◄◄◄

This is the only story in the Bible where Jesus is shown writing. But what was he writing in the dust? The Bible doesn't say. Some people believe it was the sins of the woman's accusers. Other people think it may have been the Ten Commandments. Or he might simply have been giving the accusers time to think about what they were doing and make a better choice.

When Jesus said a person without sin had to throw the first stone, he was referring to the same law of Moses the accusers were quoting at him. The law didn't mean that this person had to be completely sinless, but it had to be someone who was innocent of the crime being punished. The woman's accusers realized Jesus knew they were not innocent in this case, because they were using the situation to try to harm Jesus.

➤➤➤| HER GOD |◄◄◄

The woman in this story was guilty of a very serious sin—betraying her husband and breaking the promises she made when she got married. Jesus didn't say her sin was no big deal, but he offered her forgiveness and a second chance.

The Bible tells us the consequence of sin is death (see Romans 6:23). But Jesus stepped into our place and took that penalty for us. He took our death so we could have life. No matter what you've done in the past or will do in the future, Jesus offers you forgiveness and a fresh start. It's God's free gift to you—all you have to do is accept it.

READ ABOUT THE WOMAN CAUGHT IN SIN IN JOHN 8:1–11.

MARTHA

STRONG BELIEF

Jesus said to [Martha], "I am the resurrection and the life. The one who believes in me will live, even though they die; and whoever lives by believing in me will never die. Do you believe this?"

"Yes, Lord," she replied, "I believe that you are the Messiah, the Son of God, who is to come into the world."

JOHN 11:25–27

→»»| HER STORY |«««←

Martha sat in her kitchen, feeling numb. Friends, relatives, and neighbors filled her house, talking and weeping and fussing over Martha and her sister, Mary, but all their noise and activity were just a faint buzz on the edge of the frozen numbness that filled Martha's whole body. A small part of her mind noticed how odd it felt to be sitting still while other women bustled around her kitchen, preparing food, washing dishes, sweeping the floor, shooing children out, telling everyone where to sit and what to do. Martha was usually the one taking charge of any gathering, making sure everyone was comfortable and had plenty to eat, making sure her home was clean and welcoming, a pleasant place to be. But now all she could do was sit and stare. She wished she could cry, but tears didn't come even when sobbing relatives hugged her. She just sat, frozen, an island of still-ness amid the busyness.

She should probably check on Mary. Her sister hadn't come out of her room all day. Every now and then one of the women would knock on Mary's door, food in their hands, but they all came back shaking their heads. Martha should go knock herself, make Mary open the door, make sure she was all right. But that was silly. Mary wasn't all right, and neither was Martha. They would never be all right again.

Through the fog in her mind, the women's conversation in the kitchen caught Martha's attention. ". . . coming here! I've been wanting to hear him speak. My cousin went to hear him with her husband. They were in the middle of nowhere, and he fed all of them—more than five thousand people!—with just a few loaves of bread and some fish! My cousin swears she saw him do it!"

"I heard he cured a man who was born blind!"

"Psh!" one of Martha's aunts scoffed. "If he's so powerful, why didn't he do anything for poor Lazarus? And he was supposed to be such a good friend to him and his sisters!" The woman saw Martha watching and quickly fell silent.

"Jesus is coming?" For the first time in four days, Martha felt something.

The women looked at each other awkwardly. Finally, one of them said, "He's on his way. He's almost here."

Martha got up and ran out of the house, ignoring the calls and exclamations behind her. She needed to see Jesus. Now.

She was out of breath by the time she finally saw a group of men approaching. Jesus and his twelve disciples stopped when they noticed her. Some of the men spoke an awkward greeting, but Martha ignored them.

"Lord," she gasped, holding her hands out to Jesus, "if you had been here, my brother would not have died." She and Mary had wanted so desperately for him to come, had been sure he would appear any moment. But then Lazarus breathed for the last time, and still Jesus wasn't there. They had buried their brother, placing him on a cold stone platform in a cave-like tomb, and still Jesus wasn't there. And now here he was. Too late.

Jesus took her hands, tears filling his eyes. Martha took a shuddering breath. "But I know that even now God will give you whatever you ask." Why had she said that? What could Jesus do now? She knew he had done many miraculous things, but death couldn't be undone.

"Your brother will rise again," Jesus said, his voice gentle.

Martha nodded. "I know he will rise again in the resurrection at the last day," she said. That day felt a long way off.

Jesus squeezed her hands. "*I* am the resurrection and the life," he said, looking intently into her eyes. "The one who believes in me will live, even though they die; and whoever lives by believing in me will never die. Do you believe this, Martha?"

Martha looked into her Teacher's eyes. She wasn't exactly sure what he meant, but she knew she could trust him. Her grief and doubt and pain faded just a tiny bit, and for a moment, she knew everything would be all right, as long as Jesus was at her side. "Yes, Lord," she replied, "I believe that you are the Messiah, the Son of God."

Jesus smiled at her. He asked for Mary, and after speaking to her, asked to see where Lazarus was buried.

And then he wept.

Martha's own tears finally broke free as Jesus cried. Somehow, she felt he was mourning not just for Lazarus, but for all the death in the world, all the sadness, all the brokenness.

Martha turned, leading Jesus and the rest of the people toward Lazarus's tomb. Mary came beside Martha, and she put an arm around her sister. Jesus stood looking at the stone that covered the entrance of the tomb, deep sadness still on his tear-streaked face. "Take away the stone," he said.

Martha frowned. Had Jesus forgotten how long it had been? "But, Lord," she reminded him, "Lazarus has been in the grave for four days already. By this time, there will be a bad smell."

Jesus smiled at her again. "If you believe, you will see the glory of God."

Trust filled Martha's heart again, and she motioned for some of the men to take away the stone. She braced herself for the odor of death as the tomb was opened, but none came.

Jesus looked into the sky. "Father," he prayed loudly, "thank you for hearing me. You always hear me, but I said it out loud for the sake of all these people standing here, so they will believe you sent me." Then he took a deep breath and shouted, "Lazarus, come out!"

Martha's heart pounded. Mary gasped and clutched at her. Martha stared at Jesus—had he really ordered a dead man to walk out of his grave? But Jesus was looking at the entrance to the tomb.

Martha followed his gaze. For a few seconds, the hole in the rocky hillside was dark and empty, like it had been after they'd laid Lazarus inside the tomb. But then a shape appeared, coming slowly out into the light. A very familiar shape.

Mary cried out. Martha felt like she might faint. How could it be?

"There you are, Lazarus," Jesus said, sounding pleased. "Someone help him get those grave clothes off. He doesn't need them anymore."

Martha rushed toward her brother, wild joy and hope bursting in her chest. Death could be undone after all—by her Teacher and her Lord. Jesus truly was the resurrection and the life!

→»» | HER WORLD |«««←

Martha and her siblings were close friends with Jesus, and it seems he often stayed with them on his way to or from Jerusalem. If you've heard of Martha before, you may be more familiar with the story of a time Jesus came to her house and she got upset with her sister, Mary, for sitting down to listen to Jesus instead of helping her. Martha is known for being a hard worker and a hospitable homemaker, but her story is often told as an example of what not to do—don't get so busy you don't have time for Jesus!

Martha, like all of us, certainly had her faults, but it's clear Jesus loved her deeply. His declaration to her, "I am the resurrection and the life" (John 11:25), is one of the most famous verses in the Bible, but people often forget he said it to Martha—a woman we often look down on or shake our heads at. Jesus said those beautiful words to comfort and strengthen his friend in her grief, to give her hope. Jesus's disciple John, who recorded this story in his gospel, may have overheard the conversation between Jesus and Martha, or perhaps Martha filled him in on the details later—or maybe both! Either way, Martha is one of the Bible's important witnesses to who Jesus was.

HER GOD

Martha didn't expect Jesus to raise her brother from the dead; we can see that from her very practical objection when Jesus wanted to open Lazarus's tomb! She thought there was a dead body decaying inside that grave, and after four days it would smell terrible. But we can see from her conversation with Jesus that she trusted him—she trusted that he was the Messiah, the Savior. She knew only he could help her in her terrible sadness, even if she didn't know how.

Raising someone from the dead is an extremely special miracle—Jesus only did it a few times when he was on earth, and it's not something we expect to see or experience today. But we can know Jesus is still the resurrection and the life. Death was not the end of his story, and if we trust in him, it will not be the end of ours. Even when we come face-to-face with the worst brokenness in this messed-up world—with death itself—Jesus will be beside us, to comfort and save us. If we believe this, we will see God's glory, just as he promised Martha.

READ ABOUT MARTHA IN LUKE 10:38–42; JOHN 11:1–12:3.

Mary took about a pint of pure nard, an expensive perfume; she poured it on Jesus' feet and wiped his feet with her hair. And the house was filled with the fragrance of the perfume. . . . [Jesus said,] "She has done a beautiful thing to me. . . . She did what she could. She poured perfume on my body beforehand to prepare for my burial. Truly I tell you, wherever the gospel is preached throughout the world, what she has done will also be told, in memory of her."

JOHN 12:3; MARK 14:6, 8-9

➤➤➤| HER STORY |◄◄◄

Mary watched her sister, Martha, out of the corner of her eye as she arranged pieces of bread on a serving platter. Martha bustled here and there, scooping food into dishes, wiping surfaces, making sure everything was perfect. Mary smiled fondly at her sister. Martha loved being in charge of a kitchen and hosting events, making sure everyone was well fed and having a good time. She had been thrilled when their friend Simon asked her to serve dinner at the party he was throwing in Jesus's honor. Mary and Martha's brother, Lazarus, had become something of a celebrity in their hometown of Bethany after Jesus brought him back from the dead. The siblings had received many invitations from friends and neighbors who wanted to hear all about the miracle. Lazarus never got tired of telling the story, and Mary and Martha never got tired of watching their brother tell it—happy, healthy, and alive. And this party was all the more special because Jesus was here too, visiting Bethany on his way to Jerusalem to

A GENEROUS
WIDOW

STRENGTH TO GIVE

Calling his disciples to him, Jesus said, "Truly I tell you, this poor widow has put more into the treasury than all the others. They all gave out of their wealth; but she, out of her poverty, put in everything—all she had to live on."

MARK 12:43-44

⤞⟩⟩⟩⎸ HER STORY ⎹⟨⟨⟨⤝

Humming happily, the widow finished tidying her house and got ready to go out. Walking to the temple to give her offering was one of her favorite things to do. She was never able to give much, but she loved feeling like she was contributing in some small way to God's work. God had always taken care of her over the years, and it made her happy to honor him with a part of what he had given her.

The widow found her money box and peeked inside. Just two small coins left—and she wasn't sure when she would get more. It was difficult to make ends meet as a widow living on her own. But she had to bring something to the temple.

She took one of the coins out and tucked it safely into her coin purse. She pulled her shawl around her and headed for the door, then stopped in her tracks. Hadn't she just been thinking about how God always took care of her? She went back to the money box and took out the other coin. She chuckled as she slipped it into the coin purse. She was looking forward to seeing how God would provide!

The widow's heart felt light as she walked to the temple, calling out

WOMEN WHO FOLLOWED
AND SUPPORTED JESUS

STRONG SUPPORT

Jesus traveled about from one town and village to another, proclaiming the good news of the kingdom of God. The Twelve were with him, and also some women . . . : Mary (called Magdalene) . . . ; Joanna the wife of Chuza, the manager of Herod's household; Susanna; and many others. These women were helping to support them out of their own means. . . . Some women were watching [the crucifixion] from a distance. Among them were Mary Magdalene, Mary the mother of James the younger and of Joseph, and Salome. In Galilee these women had followed him and cared for his needs. Many other women who had come up with him to Jerusalem were also there.

LUKE 8:1-3; MARK 15:40-41

THEIR STORY

Susanna clung to her friend Joanna, soaking the shoulder of Joanna's beautiful robe with her tears. Several of their friends stood nearby, sobbing or numbly silent. Jesus's mother, Mary, had pushed closer to the cross, ignoring the other women's attempts to keep her back. Finally, Mary Magdalene and Mary the wife of Clopas had gone with her. Susanna couldn't imagine what Mary must be feeling as she watched her son suffer.

How had it come to this? Just a short time ago, the friends had been traveling with their rabbi—their Teacher, Jesus—and their fellow disciples, laughing and sharing stories along the road; making sure the whole group had enough to eat and somewhere to sleep; marveling that they, as women, were getting the chance to follow and learn from a rabbi. Who had ever heard of such a thing? They had all come to Jerusalem for the Passover celebration with such anticipation and excitement. When Jesus entered the city in what looked like a royal parade, with cheering crowds lining the streets, the friends had been sure the whole world was realizing what they had believed for a long time—that Jesus was the Messiah, God's Anointed One, sent to deliver their people.

But now they were on a rocky hill outside Jerusalem, watching from a distance as their beloved Teacher was executed by the worst form of torture the Romans knew—crucifixion. They had nailed Jesus's hands and feet to a wooden cross, and he would hang there until he died of suffocation. It was a terrible death that could drag on for days. Susanna wouldn't wish it on the worst kind of criminal—it was unthinkable for her gentle, kind, and loving rabbi.

Agonizing hours passed. The women grew exhausted from fear and grief as well as from standing, but none of them left. They would stay with their Teacher until the end.

At long last, it was over. Jesus was dead.

Joanna went to speak to a group of their friends. "Joseph of Arimathea will ask the governor if he can take down Jesus's body," she told Susanna when she returned. "He and Nicodemus will put the Teacher in Joseph's tomb and do what they can to prepare his body before the sun goes down."

Susanna had forgotten it was almost the Sabbath. No one could do any work after sunset, according to Jewish law.

"Some of us women will go to the tomb early in the morning on the day after the Sabbath to finish the burial," Joanna said. "Come with me now—I want to see if we can buy burial spices before the market closes." Her eyes filled with tears. "It's the last thing I will do for the Teacher."

Susanna took her friend's hand and squeezed it. Together, the women hurried away to perform their final act of love.

THEIR WORLD

In Bible times, Jewish teachers—called rabbis—would have a group of students that followed them and learned from them. These students, or disciples, would listen to everything the rabbi said and try to be like the rabbi. If you've heard or read stories about Jesus, you're probably familiar with his twelve disciples (who are also known as the twelve apostles). These men were Jesus's closest followers and friends.

The Bible tells us many women also traveled with Jesus. Some of these women supported Jesus and his followers with their own money—paying for food, lodging, and other necessities as they traveled. These women helped make it possible for Jesus to teach, heal people, and do the work God had for him. Jesus welcomed these women into his world—the kingdom of God.

THEIR GOD

Jesus called together a group of followers, and he taught them to love not just him but each other (see John 15:12). Throughout the Bible, we see God doesn't just call certain individuals but groups of people. In the Old Testament, God made a special covenant with the nation of Israel. Then in the New Testament, Jesus called his followers and made a new covenant with them. These men and women eventually became the Christian Church.

Jesus still wants his followers and friends to love, serve, and care for one another. Church isn't just a building—it's a family! We show love to Jesus when we love one another.

> READ ABOUT THE WOMEN WHO FOLLOWED AND SUPPORTED JESUS IN MATTHEW 27:55–61; 28:1–10; MARK 15:40–41; 16:1–11; LUKE 8:2–3; 24:1–12; JOHN 19:25–27.

MARY MAGDALENE

THE STRENGTH IN A NAME

[Mary] turned to leave and saw someone standing there. It was Jesus, but she didn't recognize him. "Dear woman, why are you crying?" Jesus asked her. "Who are you looking for?"

She thought he was the gardener. "Sir," she said, "if you have taken him away, tell me where you have put him, and I will go and get him."

"Mary!" Jesus said.

She turned to him and cried out, "Rabboni!" (which is Hebrew for "Teacher").

JOHN 20:14–16, NLT

HER STORY

Mary raced down the road, her feet pounding the packed dirt, sweat running down her temples despite the early morning chill. She could hear her friends panting and stumbling behind her, but she didn't wait. Her mind whirled with grief and confusion.

Ignoring the pain in her sides, Mary didn't stop until she reached the house where the Twelve were staying. She pounded on the door. Some of her friends had caught up and stood behind her, gasping for air.

The door was yanked open, and Peter and John stood there, eyes wide and faces wary.

"They have taken the Lord away from his tomb!" Mary gasped. "We don't know where they have put him!" She poured out the whole story, her friends interjecting here and there. About how they had gone to the tomb before dawn, carrying spices to complete Jesus's burial. How they had wondered along the way how they would move the huge stone Joseph of Arimathea had placed in the tomb's entrance. How they had arrived to find the stone rolled away and the Roman soldiers who had been assigned to guard the tomb scattered on the ground, stunned and shaken. How two men had been there, dressed in dazzling clothes, and their incredible words: "Why are you looking for the living among the dead?"

As the women told their story, other disciples appeared, crowding behind Peter and John. They shook their heads in confusion and disbelief. "Grave robbers probably stole the body," one of them murmured. "That's the last thing we need."

"But what about the men who spoke to them?" someone else asked.

A third man shook his head. "The women have been through a terrible experience. That plus the shock of finding the body gone . . . Maybe they imagined it."

Mary felt a stab of frustration. She and the other women had all seen and heard the same things. They might not understand what was happening, but they hadn't imagined it.

"We'd better go see the tomb," Peter said. "Come on, John." Peter and John took off at a run. The other disciples and the women looked at one another for a few minutes. But Mary turned and set off in the direction Peter and John had gone. She needed to see everything for herself again.

By the time she got back to the tomb, Peter and John had left. All the sadness and fear of the last three days and the shock of the morning broke over Mary at once, like a crashing wave, and she began to cry.

After a few minutes, she bent to look into the tomb again, peering through the darkness and her tears. The two men in dazzling clothes were there! One of them sat at each end of the platform where Jesus's body had been. "Dear woman, why are you crying?" they asked.

"They have taken my Lord away," Mary sobbed, "and I don't know where they have put him!"

A noise behind her made her spin. A man stood there—likely one of the gardeners who took care of the area around the tomb. "Dear woman, why are you crying?" the man asked. "Who are you looking for?"

"Sir," Mary sniffled, "if you took the body away, just tell me where he is, and I will go get him." Jesus was gone, and she hadn't even been able to help bury him properly! She turned away, concealing her face in her hands.

"Mary!"

She knew that voice! She had first heard it calling to her through the noise of the seven evil spirits that once lived inside her. That voice had cut through the confusion and torment, sent the demons away, and brought Mary back to herself. She had heard it loud while teaching crowds on a hillside, and soft while speaking tenderly to a child. It was the dearest voice to Mary, and she had thought she would never hear it again.

She whirled around, her eyes confirming what her ears already knew. Jesus was standing there—solid and alive and smiling at her. "Rabboni!" she cried out in joy. *My teacher!*

She rushed toward him, fell at his feet, and wrapped her arms around his legs, feeling like she might never let go. "Don't cling to me," Jesus said, a hint of laughter in his voice. "I haven't gone up to the Father yet. Go find the disciples, my brothers, and tell them I am going up to my Father and your Father, my God and your God."

Mary got up reluctantly, but looking into Jesus's face, she felt in her heart that she would never lose him again. Full of joy, she rushed back the way she had come and pounded on the door for the second time that day. "I have seen the Lord!" she shouted at the astonished faces that greeted her. "Jesus is alive!"

⇢⟫⟩| HER WORLD |⟨⟨⟨⟵

Mary and the other women went to the tomb early that Sunday morning to finish Jesus's burial. (Jesus died on a Friday evening, and Saturday was the Sabbath—the Jewish day of rest where nobody could do any work—so Sunday was the earliest they could go.) In Israel at the time, it was common to bury people in above-ground tombs. A dead body would be placed on a platform until only the skeleton was left. Then the bones would be put into a small compartment of the tomb. This way multiple people (often family members) could be buried in the same grave. Fragrant spices were used to cover the odor of the decaying body. Nicodemus wrapped Jesus's body with spices when he and Joseph took him down from the cross and placed him in the tomb, but they were in a hurry to get Jesus into the tomb before the Sabbath began, so the women were likely going to finish the job.

According to Jewish law, women were not considered reliable witnesses. Testimony could not be used in court unless it came from two or more men. That's likely why the disciples didn't believe the women and sent Peter and John to investigate. Many people point to the fact that women were the first witnesses of Jesus's resurrection as proof it really happened, because if someone were making up the story, they wouldn't have had "unreliable" people be the first to see Jesus alive.

→»»| HER GOD |«««-

Over the centuries, many people have been curious about Mary Magdalene, and many stories, legends, and traditions have been made up about her. People wonder how she came to be possessed by seven demons; and some believe she must have been a very sinful person. But the Bible doesn't tell us very much about Mary, only that Jesus saved her from evil spirits and that she was one of his followers. She was near Jesus's cross when he died and went to his tomb that Sunday morning. And she was one of the first people Jesus appeared to and spoke to after his resurrection.

But Jesus knew all about Mary. And when he spoke her name, she knew him. Jesus called himself the Good Shepherd who knows each of his sheep, and his sheep know his voice (see John 10:27). If you are one of Jesus's sheep, he knows your name and everything about you. As you follow him, his voice will become more familiar to you every day.

READ ABOUT MARY MAGDALENE IN MATTHEW 27:56, 61; 28:1; MARK 15:40, 47; 16:1–19; LUKE 8:2; 24:10; JOHN 19:25; 20:1–18.

TABITHA

A STRONG LEGACY

There was a disciple named Tabitha (in Greek her name is Dorcas); she was always doing good and helping the poor.

ACTS 9:36

→»»| HER STORY |«««-

Tabitha put her needle down with a sigh and closed her eyes. She just needed a moment to rest. Today, she was feeling unusually tired, but she could rest only for a moment because she needed to finish the clothes for the widows in her community. Tabitha loved to do what she could for them because she knew the widows' lives were hard, especially if they had young children. She also made a point of getting to know the other people around her who were struggling, paying attention to what they needed and helping in whatever way she could. Jesus had said doing good for the poor was like doing good for him; she loved to think she was serving Jesus with every piece of clothing she made and every meal she cooked.

If only she wasn't so tired today! Actually, she wasn't feeling well at all, if she was being honest. Tabitha wondered if she was coming down with something. But she couldn't be sick! She had so much to do . . .

Days later, Tabitha still wasn't well. In fact, she feeling weaker every minute. Was it truly her time to die? She didn't feel like her work on earth was done, not even close, but she supposed if Jesus was calling, she would trust him and go.

"Tabitha, get up."

She opened her eyes. She was lying on a bed in a room that seemed

207

familiar and yet strange. She was in her room, in her house, but a moment ago she had been somewhere else.

There was a man kneeling by her bed. She sat up in surprise. It was Peter, one of Jesus's twelve closest followers! Peter took her by the hand and helped her stand. "There are a lot of people who are anxious to see you," he said, smiling. He stuck his head out of the door. "Come!" he called. "Here is Tabitha! She's alive!"

People crowded into the room: Tabitha's friends and neighbors, widows she'd helped. They gathered around her, laughing and crying.

Tabitha hugged her friends and smiled. It seemed her work on earth wasn't done yet after all.

→»»| HER WORLD |«««–

After Jesus's resurrection, he spent forty days on earth. At the end of that time, he went up—or ascended—into heaven, his mission on earth complete. One of the last instructions he gave his followers before his ascension was to teach other people about who he was and what he had done so others could become his followers too. Jesus's friends, led by the twelve disciples, traveled to many places to tell people the good news about Jesus. Jesus's disciple Peter was on one of these mission trips when this story took place.

Tabitha—also known by her Greek name, Dorcas—lived in a town called Joppa. She was beloved in her community for everything she did to help the poor there. When Tabitha got sick and died, her friends begged Peter to see if he could help. Peter came to the house where Tabitha was, and was met by all the widows Tabitha had helped, crying and showing him the clothes she had made for them. Peter sent everyone out of the room and knelt to pray. Then he told Tabitha to get up, and she came back to life! Many people heard about this amazing miracle Peter did through the power of Jesus and decided to follow Jesus too.

Tabitha lived by Jesus's words in Matthew 25:40: "Truly I tell you, whatever you did for one of the least of these brothers and sisters of mine, you did for me." She showed love to Jesus by showing love to the people around her who needed it most. Serving others is often hard and almost never exciting or glamorous, but it makes Jesus very happy. Jesus set the ultimate example of how to serve with love, and he calls us to follow him in service (see John 13:12–17). Acts of service don't have to be big or dramatic. There are many ways we can serve the people near us—starting with our own families and then our community. Each act of service is an act of love to God.

READ ABOUT TABITHA IN ACTS 9:36–43.

LYDIA

STRONG HOSPITALITY

One of those listening [to Paul] was a woman from the
city of Thyatira named Lydia, a dealer in purple cloth. She
was a worshiper of God. The Lord opened her heart to
respond to Paul's message. When she and the members
of her household were baptized, she invited [Paul and his
companions] to her home. "If you consider me a believer in
the Lord," she said, "come and stay at my house."

ACTS 16:14–15

⟶⟩⟩⟩| HER STORY |⟨⟨⟨⟵

Lydia took a deep breath, enjoying the fresh morning air as she walked
down to the Gangites River, her family and servants trailing behind her.
She joined this Sabbath meeting with other worshipers of God whenever her business brought her to Philippi. The sky was overcast today, the
clouds nearly as purple as the beautiful cloth Lydia sold to her wealthy
customers. She hoped the rain would hold off until after the meeting.

Lydia arrived at the meeting place and greeted the other women
gathered there. There weren't enough Jewish men in Philippi to form a
synagogue, so the group met in this peaceful spot by the river. Lydia and
her friends chatted while they waited for everyone to arrive.

Lydia was talking to a friend when she noticed the woman looking
past her. Glancing over her shoulder to see what had caught her friend's
attention, Lydia saw several men approaching the gathering. She could
tell they were Jewish, but she'd never seen them before. The men greeted
the women politely, then one asked if he could speak to everyone. He

introduced himself as Paul, a Pharisee and rabbi from the city of Tarsus. The women whispered excitedly. It wasn't every day their small group was able to hear from a rabbi! They eagerly invited him to begin.

Paul and his companions sat down, and the rabbi began to speak. Lydia listened, fascinated. She had never heard any of the Jews or Gentile believers in God say things like this man did! Some of it sounded incredible, but as she heard more, she felt God speaking to her heart, assuring her that everything Paul said was true. Next to her, her family and servants sat perfectly still, not taking their eyes off Paul.

By the time Paul finished, Lydia knew she believed that the Teacher he spoke of, Jesus of Nazareth, was God's Messiah, and she wanted him to be her Savior and Lord. When Paul asked if anyone wanted to be baptized, washed in water to show they were beginning a new life as a follower of Jesus, Lydia immediately stood up. She and her household, family members and servants alike, were all baptized there in the river.

Lydia felt fresh and full of joy. She thanked God for sending Paul and his companions to the river that day to bring her and her friends such wonderful news. She wanted to help Paul and his friends in their mission to tell as many people about Jesus as possible. She had a big house in Philippi—it would be the perfect home base for Paul and the others while they were in the city. They could stay there and use it for meetings.

She extended her invitation to the visitors, and they accepted. She led her household and her guests back to her house, a different woman from when she'd left home that morning.

→»»| HER WORLD |«««←

Lydia was a businesswoman—the Bible says she sold purple cloth. Purple was an extremely expensive color in the ancient world. It was made from sea snails, and it took thousands of snails to make enough dye for a single piece of cloth. The process was so long and difficult (and smelly!) that purple dye was as valuable then as diamonds are today. Purple cloth was considered so precious that the Roman Empire had laws about who was allowed to wear it. Lydia's customers were likely extremely wealthy and influential people, and Lydia herself was probably quite well off.

The city of Thyatira, where Lydia was from, was known for its cloth business. It's likely Lydia had a home there as well as in Philippi. Philippi was a major city in the area, so perhaps Lydia traveled there frequently for business.

If you've read the Bible or spent much time in church, you've probably heard of the apostle Paul. Paul was an early and famous missionary—someone who makes it their *mission* to tell people the good news about Jesus. He traveled all over the Roman Empire, preaching and starting churches. (You can read more about Paul in the book of Acts, starting in Acts 7:58.)

->»»| HER GOD |««-

Lydia had a significant impact on Paul's mission in Philippi by providing him and his fellow missionaries with a place to stay and to hold meetings where Paul could preach. Her hospitality would also have meant the group wouldn't have to worry about food or lodging expenses for as long as they were in Philippi. This was important, because Paul often had to work to support himself and his companions as they traveled. In Philippi, he was probably able to focus on preaching full time, thanks to Lydia's generosity.

It's also possible Lydia was able to take the good news to places Paul couldn't go. Paul had wanted to preach in the Roman province of Asia but hadn't been able to (see Acts 16:6). But when he went where God was leading him, he met Lydia, who was from that province—and able to bring news of Jesus to her homeland.

Paul didn't know God was going to use Lydia to meet so many needs before he got to Philippi. He just had to follow God's lead and trust God would take care of the rest. God is always at work. All we need to do is listen to his voice and follow where he leads.

> READ ABOUT LYDIA IN ACTS 16:12-15, 40.

Some of the people [of Athens] became followers of Paul and believed. Among them was Dionysius, a member of the Areopagus, also a woman named Damaris, and a number of others.

ACTS 17:34

→»»| HER STORY |«««-

The Areopagus, the high council of the city of Athens, was in session. Voices raised in debate floated over the murmurs and comments of the onlookers. Damaris lingered at the edge of the crowd, trying to find a good vantage point where she could see and hear without being noticed. She had been passing by when a name caught her attention, a name she'd heard mentioned in marketplace chatter and neighborhood gossip—Paul of Tarsus. She had heard bits and pieces of his teaching, and it had intrigued her enough that when she heard his name called out, she'd stopped in her tracks.

There! She found a convenient alcove where she could hear what the council was saying and see the speakers if she craned her neck around the corner. She listened for a moment. It seemed Paul himself was going to speak! The council wanted to hear the new ideas he'd been teaching so they could decide if they would allow him to continue to speak publicly in Athens. This was the perfect opportunity for Damaris to hear him and form her own opinion.

Paul stood up. "People of Athens!" he called out in a strong voice. He seemed calm and relaxed, someone who was used to public speaking and

even enjoyed it. "I can see that you are very religious. As I walked around the city and looked carefully at all your shrines and religious objects, I even found an altar that said, 'To an Unknown God.'" Damaris had seen that altar. Every time she passed it, she felt a hunger in her spirit, a longing to know the unknown. "This God, whom you worship without knowing," Paul continued. "I'm about to tell you about him."

Damaris gasped. It was almost as if Paul had read her mind! She listened intently as Paul continued speaking, telling the crowd about the God who gave life to all people and met all their needs, who didn't need service or offerings from humans but wanted people to know him. Who was so full of life that he could even raise the dead.

When Paul spoke of the resurrection of the dead, the council members stopped listening. Most of them made fun of Paul, though some said they wanted to hear more later. The crowd burst into a riot of noise and confusion as everyone started talking at once, commenting and arguing about what they'd just heard.

Damaris slipped away from the crowd and hurried home, her mind spinning and her heart burning inside her. She knew that after today, she would never be the same.

->>>| HER WORLD |<<<-

We know almost nothing about Damaris—she's only mentioned in one verse of the Bible, and it really only tells us her name and that she became a believer in Jesus when Paul was in Athens. There are many different ideas about who Damaris was. Some people believe that even though respectable Athenian women were often well educated, they would not have been allowed to listen to or participate in public speeches or debates. So they conclude Damaris must have either been a foreigner to Athens or a woman with a bad reputation. Other people point out that even though the Bible mentions Damaris becoming a believer in Jesus right after Paul's famous speech at the Areopagus council, it doesn't exactly say Damaris heard the speech. It's possible she heard Paul's preaching some other way. Still other people think that maybe the rules for Athenian women were not so strict and some women may have been listening in the crowd. They believe Damaris must have been an influential citizen of Athens, just like Dionysius, the council member who also believed in Jesus (some think she was Dionysius's wife). Yet another idea is that Damaris belonged to one of Athens' groups of philosophers. It's thought that one of the groups occasionally accepted women as members.

→»»| HER GOD |«««-

The one thing we can know for sure about Damaris is that she believed in Jesus. It's likely that, like many of her fellow Athenians, she had a curious mind and was very interested in knowledge and truth. The Bible tells us God is rich in wisdom and knowledge (see Romans 11:33) and he gives wisdom and shows truth to people who honestly ask for them (see James 1:5; 2 Timothy 2:25).

Do you have questions about God or the Christian life or how the world works—or all the above? God is waiting to listen to your questions and help you find answers. He shared his truth with us through his Word (see John 17:17), and he can give us more experienced and knowledgeable people who can help us. Stay curious about God—he wants you to know him!

> READ ABOUT DAMARIS IN ACTS 17:34.

PRISCILLA

STRONG TEACHING

Paul left Athens and went to Corinth. There he met a Jew named Aquila, a native of Pontus, who had recently come from Italy with his wife Priscilla. . . . Paul went to see them, and because he was a tentmaker as they were, he stayed and worked with them.

ACTS 18:1–3

⇥⟫⟫| HER STORY |⟪⟪⟪⇤

Priscilla stitched quickly, her mind as busy as her needle as she listened to the visitor who had appeared at her and her husband's leatherworking shop this morning. Their guest, Paul, was a follower of Jesus, like Priscilla and her husband, Aquila. Paul was traveling around the Roman Empire telling people about Jesus. He was also a tentmaker and leatherworker like Priscilla and Aquila, and he had come to their shop looking for work to earn money for his travels. Now he was demonstrating his skills with leather while telling them the story of how he had gone from hating followers of Jesus and trying to put them in prison to being a Jesus-follower himself.

Priscilla's eyes widened as Paul described how he had actually met Jesus on the road. A bright light had shone all around him, and Jesus had spoken to him! It must have been incredible—and terrifying! Priscilla listened closely, thanking God for the opportunity to hear from someone who had met Jesus in person. She was sure she could learn a lot from Paul.

Paul finished the piece he was working on and handing it to Aquila for inspection. Aquila looked at it carefully, then passed it to Priscilla for her

opinion. She could see right away that Paul's craftsmanship was as good as his speaking. She met Aquila's eyes and nodded her approval. It would be wonderful to work with another experienced tentmaker for a while. But even better was the opportunity to hear Paul speak about Jesus every day!

Years later, Priscilla looked around at the church gathered in her and Aquila's home and marveled at the amazing journey God had brought them on. They had taken a literal journey, joining Paul when he left Corinth and traveling with him as far as Ephesus, where they had lived for a while. Eventually, they had been able to return to their old home in Rome. She and her husband had learned so much about how to follow Jesus, both from Paul's teaching and the experiences God had brought their way. Priscilla and Aquila had been given the chance to teach others as well. And now they were leading a church in their home.

Priscilla looked from face to face, some beloved and familiar, some new and curious. She smiled at Aquila as he stood and welcomed everyone. She couldn't wait to see what God would do next!

->>>| HER WORLD |<<<-

Priscilla and Aquila were Jews who lived outside the land of Israel. The Bible says Aquila was from the Roman province of Pontus. Priscilla and Aquila lived in Rome at one point, but they had to leave when the emperor decided to kick all Jews out of the city. Priscilla and Aquila were living in the Greek city of Corinth when they met the apostle Paul. It's likely Priscilla and Aquila were already followers of Jesus when they met Paul. The three of them had the same job, tentmaking (tentmakers at the time made and repaired all kinds of leather items). Paul may have sought out Priscilla and Aquila because he needed to work and make money for his travels, or perhaps he heard they were followers of Jesus, or both!

Paul lived with Priscilla and Aquila in Corinth for about a year and a half, then they joined him when he continued his journey. Eventually, they settled in the city of Ephesus (in modern-day Turkey). Sometime after that, they returned to Rome, where a church met in their home. Then they ultimately went back to Ephesus.

Paul wrote many letters to churches he met or helped form during his travels. Many of these letters became books of the Bible (sometimes they're known as the Pauline Epistles). Paul mentions Priscilla and Aquila several times in his letters.

When Priscilla and Aquila are mentioned in the Bible, Priscilla's name usually comes first, which was unusual for the time. That might be because Priscilla came from a higher social class than Aquila, or because she was more famous in the church for some other reason.

→»»| HER GOD |««←-

The Bible doesn't give many details about Priscilla's life, but one clear theme we can see in her story is partnership. She and her husband, Aquila, are always mentioned together—they worked together, traveled together, and taught together. They partnered with Paul to help him continue his work, and they likely learned from him while he was with them, better preparing them for the mission God had planned.

God is always bringing his people together to help, strengthen, and encourage one another. He wants us to be there for one another and build each other up (see 1 Thessalonians 5:11). We are stronger together!

> READ ABOUT PRISCILLA IN ACTS 18:2, 18, 26;
> ROMANS 16:3; 1 CORINTHIANS 16:19; 2 TIMOTHY 4:19.

WOMEN
IN THE CHURCH

A CHURCH'S STRENGTH

I [Paul] commend to you our sister Phoebe. . . . Welcome her in the Lord as one who is worthy of honor among God's people. . . . Give my greetings to Priscilla and Aquila, my co-workers in the ministry of Christ Jesus. . . . Give my greetings to Mary . . . and Junia . . . to Tryphena and Tryphosa, the Lord's workers, and to dear Persis, who has worked so hard for the Lord. Greet Rufus . . . and also his dear mother, who has been a mother to me. . . . Give my greetings to . . . Julia, Nereus and his sister.

ROMANS 16:1–3, 6–7, 12–13, 15, NLT

⟶≫| THEIR STORY |≪⟵

Phoebe settled into a comfortable seat and smiled at her hostess, Priscilla. "Let me get you something to eat and drink," Priscilla said, already bustling around, filling a tray with delicious-looking dishes. "It will be a while before people begin to arrive. Everyone will be so happy to read the letter you've brought."

Phoebe looked at the bag containing the heavy document she'd just delivered to Priscilla and Aquila's house. It was a long letter from Paul to the churches in Rome. Once the church that met in this house read it, they would pass it on to another, who would pass it on in turn, until everyone had a chance to read Paul's teaching and messages. Phoebe was happy to have completed her mission and delivered the letter safely. She'd met Paul at her home in Cenchrea, near Corinth. She'd had the opportunity to

support him there, and when he'd heard she would be traveling to Rome, he'd asked her to carry his letter with her.

Later, Phoebe looked around the room at the church gathered in Priscilla and Aquila's house. They'd been listening closely for a long time as Aquila read Paul's letter aloud. It contained a lot of valuable teaching about Jesus and how to live as his followers, and Phoebe knew she would be thinking about the things Paul had written for a long time. Now they had finally come to the end of the letter, where Paul had written some personal greetings.

First was a kind introduction from Paul of Phoebe herself, asking the Roman church to welcome her and treat her well. Aquila looked up and smiled at Phoebe as he read. Then Paul sent greetings to Priscilla and Aquila and the group meeting in their house. As Aquila read out more greetings, Phoebe was struck by the number of female names—Mary, Junia, Tryphena, Tryphosa, Persis, Julia. It reminded her how different life in the church was from the life she'd known before. She hadn't met many well-known men like Paul who would gladly recognize women as his fellow workers. She knew women played important roles in her own home church, and it was obvious that was the case here in Rome as well. It felt good to hear Paul recognize that, and she knew that in doing so he was following Jesus's example.

→»»| THEIR WORLD |«««-

The book of Romans is the longest letter Paul wrote, and it contains very important truths about Jesus and the Christian life. Paul likely wrote the letter during one of his missionary journeys, probably while he was staying in Corinth. Cenchrea, where Phoebe was from, was very close to Corinth. Phoebe's name means "bright," and is Latin, which may mean she was a Gentile believer—or she may have been a Jew who also had a Latin name, like Paul. From the way Paul describes Phoebe in Romans, it's likely she was a wealthy woman who helped provide for Paul's needs. Paul calls Phoebe a "deacon" of her church, using the Greek word *diakonos*. That word could refer to someone who had the office of deacon—similar to deacons in many churches today—or it could simply mean a "servant" of the church. Either way, Phoebe played an important and influential role in her church.

Paul mentions ten women in his personal greetings at the end of the letter to the Roman church, eight by name (Phoebe, Priscilla, Mary, Junia, Tryphena, Tryphosa, Persis, and Julia) and two by their relation to someone else (Rufus's mother and Nereus's sister). Aside from Priscilla, the women are mentioned only in this chapter, and we don't know much about them. Junia was likely married to Andronicus, since their names are linked together, and Tryphena and Tryphosa were likely sisters, since their names are so similar. But the Bible doesn't tell us that for sure.

→»»| THEIR GOD |«««←

What we can know for certain about the women of Romans 16 is that they were important to Paul—and to Jesus. They clearly did meaningful and important work for God and their fellow believers. Nearly every time Paul says something about a woman apart from her name, it is that she was helpful, a worker or coworker, or worked hard. And he says Junia was "highly respected"—it's possible she was a missionary like him or had some kind of leadership role in the church.

You don't have to wait to get older, smarter, or better known to do important work for God. Ask him to show you ways you can serve him and his Church right where you are with the talents and strengths he's given you. That may mean doing jobs that seem boring and small and don't get much praise or recognition. But God loves to reward good work that goes unrecognized by the world (see Matthew 6:1–6). He has a vital role for you to play.

> READ ABOUT WOMEN IN THE CHURCH IN ROMANS 16.

LOIS AND EUNICE

STRONG MOTHERS

You share the faith that first filled your grandmother Lois and your mother, Eunice.

2 TIMOTHY 1:5, NLT

->》》| THEIR STORY |《《《-

Eunice kneaded more flour into her dough, the familiar motions of making bread soothing her mind and heart. She often prayed silently to the rhythm of her kneading, and usually her prayers were for her son, Timothy, who was serving God and his Church far away.

Eunice's mother, Lois, wiped dishes nearby, softly singing a psalm. Eunice smiled, remembering the hours she'd spent as a little girl learning the Hebrew Scriptures from her. When Eunice had her own child, she passed that knowledge on to him, with Lois's help. When Eunice and Lois became followers of Jesus, they had taught Timothy to love him too. He'd grown strong in the faith the same way he'd grown up physically, and everyone in their area liked and respected him.

Eunice would never forget the day the apostle Paul came to their town. Timothy had come home full of excitement, eager to learn everything the missionary had to teach. Paul and Timothy grew close, and Paul invited her son to join him on his travels. Eunice smiled at the memory of Timothy setting off on his journey, nervousness and enthusiasm all over his face, ready to begin the work Jesus wanted him to do. Eunice and Lois had cried as they watched him walk away, and they still missed him every moment, but they were trusting Jesus to care for him, just as they had ever since he was born.

→»»| THEIR WORLD |«««-

We don't know much about these two women, who Paul mentions in his second letter to his protégée Timothy. Their names appear in only one verse of the Bible, though Eunice is mentioned as Timothy's mother in another passage. But the Bible does tell us some important things about them.

Timothy was a church leader and missionary, and very close to the Bible's most famous missionary, Paul. His mother, Eunice, was a Jewish woman who had become a believer in Jesus. Timothy's father was Greek, and that's all we know about him. Some people think he may have died by the time Timothy met Paul, since Paul became a father figure to Timothy. In fact, Paul called Timothy his "true son in the faith" (1 Timothy 1:2). But Paul knew Timothy had first learned how to be a Christian from Eunice and Lois, his mother and grandmother. Lois and Eunice did such a good job passing their faith on to Timothy that Paul mentions them by name in this letter, the last one he wrote to Timothy. Paul knew his work on earth was almost over, and in this letter he gives Timothy the job of taking over where he left off. He tells Timothy to remember what he learned from his mother and grandmother as he takes on this huge task.

→»»| THEIR GOD |«««-

Lois and Eunice likely had very ordinary lives. They probably didn't feel that different from the other mothers they knew. But it's clear they knew a mother's most important job is to teach her children about God. And it's clear they did that job very well.

We often call God our Father, and that's a good thing—the Bible tells us God is our heavenly Father. But the Bible uses some images, or word pictures, that show us God is also like a mother. God tells us he is like a mother bird who protects her babies under her wings (see Psalm 91:4; Matthew 23:37) and like a mother eagle who teaches her babies how to fly (see Deuteronomy 32:11). He also says he is like a human mother who loves and comforts her child (see Isaiah 49:15; 66:13).

Remember, God made both men and women in his image. These verses tell us that good mothers as well as good fathers reflect characteristics and aspects of God.

READ ABOUT LOIS AND EUNICE IN 2 TIMOTHY 1:5.

THE WOMAN
CROWNED WITH STARS

A STRONG SYMBOL

A great sign appeared in heaven: a woman clothed with the sun, with the moon under her feet and a crown of twelve stars on her head.

REVELATION 12:1

→»»| HER STORY |«««←

A loud cry of pain echoed across the heavens as the woman standing on the moon doubled over in pain, wrapping her arms around her round, stretched belly. Brilliant beams of sunlight wove around her, forming a golden robe, and twelve stars glittered in the crown on her head. Another wave of pain made her clench her fists, nails digging into her palms. Her baby would arrive very soon.

The woman's next cry was answered by a chorus of low, hungry growls. A huge red dragon lurked in front of her, all seven of its horned, crowned heads snapping their jaws. The dragon lashed his tail, sweeping a third of the stars from the sky and sending them crashing to earth. It growled again, waiting to devour the woman's baby the moment it was born.

With her loudest cry yet, the woman delivered a baby boy. The seven red, scaly heads lunged forward, mouths opened wide, but the baby was whisked away to safety—to God's own throne.

Roaring with rage, the dragon turned on the mother, but God had prepared a refuge for her as well. She fled into the wilderness, where the dragon couldn't reach her.

Furious at being deprived of his prey, the dragon started an epic battle

in heaven. An army of angels, led by their captain—an archangel named Michael—fought the dragon and his fallen angels. Michael's forces defeated the dragon's army, flinging them out of heaven and down to earth.

A loud voice boomed out across the heavens: "At last! Here are salvation and power, God's Kingdom and the reign of his Messiah. The accuser of our brothers and sisters has been thrown down to earth, defeated by the blood of the Lamb of God and the testimony of those who believe in him. They were not afraid to die. Be joyful, everyone in heaven! But watch out, earth—the dragon is furious, because he doesn't have much time."

The dragon picked himself up from the ground and shook himself. He opened his seven mouths and bellowed with anger. Then he began to hunt the woman with the crown of stars. But she was given the wings of a great eagle so she could escape. Next, the dragon spewed a huge flood of water out of his mouth to drown the woman, but the earth opened its mouth and swallowed the deluge.

The dragon gave a final huge roar of rage and frustration. He declared war on the woman's other children: everyone who follows God's ways and calls themselves followers of Jesus.

→»»| HER WORLD |«««←

The last book of the Bible, Revelation, is a book of prophecy. It records a supernatural vision that God gave to John, one of Jesus's disciples. It is full of symbols, and it can be hard to know exactly what they mean. In fact, it's confused readers almost since the time it was written.

The woman in this book is a personification, or a symbol of an important truth. Some Bible scholars believe the woman crowned with stars represents the people of Israel, while others think she is a symbol of the Christian church (and still others think she represents both—God's people throughout the ages). Some people interpret her as Jesus's mother, Mary, and this scene is sort of a picture of what was going on in the supernatural realm when Jesus was born.

The baby boy does seem to be Jesus, since he is described as the ruler of all nations (see Revelation 12:5). And the Bible directly says the red dragon is Satan, the "ancient serpent" who tempted Eve to sin and who is still the greatest enemy of God's people (see Revelation 12:9). (There are various ideas about what the dragon's heads, horns, and crowns symbolize—you can find out more by looking in Bible reference books or talking to pastors, teachers, and other people who are knowledgeable about the Bible.)

→»»| HER GOD |«««-

Though there are different ideas and interpretations about what exactly the incredible images in this story symbolize, we can know one thing for sure—God wins. As huge and scary as the evil dragon seems, he is easily defeated by God's forces. The dragon comes after the woman again and again, but God saves her every time.

What does that mean for you and me? No matter how terrible or ugly evil gets, in our lives or in the world, God will defeat it. No matter how big the danger we may face, we are safe under God's protection. The joyful call ringing out across the heavens is for us, those who have become friends of Jesus, those God calls his own: our enemy will be defeated. Our salvation is near. The Kingdom of God is coming.

> READ MORE ABOUT THE WOMAN CROWNED
> WITH STARS IN REVELATION 12.